TRAINS

by

Rixon Bucknall

GROSSET & DUNLAP
A National General Company
Publishers · New York

Managing Editor Peter Usborne
Editors Su Swallow, Susan Ellis, Chris Milsome
Illustrators Robert Corrall
　　　　　　Brian Hiley
　　　　　　William Hobson
　　　　　　Frank Friend
　　　　　　Tony Mitchell
　　　　　　Jack Pelling
Illustrations consultant John W. Wood
Projects R. H. Warring
Picture research Marion Gain, Ann Usborne

Information and assistance were also given by
The German Tourist Information Bureau, London,
The Japanese Embassy Information Section, London,
The Japanese National Tourist Organization, London,
The Science Museum, London.

Published in the United States by
Grosset & Dunlap, Inc.
New York, N.Y.

1973 PRINTING

contents

Library of Congress Catalog Card Number: 72-161542
ISBN: 0-448-00726-6 (Trade Edition)
ISBN: 0-448-03534-0 (Library Edition)

Steam pioneers

Steam pumps

The first trains were pulled along by horses. These horse-drawn trains of the 1760's were used in industry. Passengers were not carried on railroads until 1804, after the first steam locomotive was built.

The first steam engine of any kind, however, was not built to pull trains. It was coal mining that led to the discovery of the steam engine. More coal was needed for use in industry, but the deep mines often flooded and could not be worked. Then in 1712 Newcomen, an Englishman, produced a steam pump which was to keep the mines dry.

James Watt, a Scotsman, built more powerful steam engines from 1775. They were used to drive factory machinery.

The first railroad engine

It was not until the nineteenth century that a steam engine was made to go on the road. Cugnot, a Frenchman, had made a steam tractor in 1769, but it was not a great success. Then in England in 1801 Richard Trevithick made a steam engine that could run on the road.

Finally, three years later, Trevithick built the first railroad engine. This engine pulled the first self-propelled train in the world. The train carried ten tons of iron and about 70 people. It traveled over nine and a half miles of tracks in South Wales. The railroad age had begun at last.

Rails

By the time the railroad engine was made, rails had been in use for several hundreds of years. Long ago, the Romans had laid two parallel lines of paving slabs along their roads for the chariot wheels to run on.

In the sixteenth century wagons were used in mining districts to carry coal. The horse-drawn wagons needed a smooth surface to run on. Wagon ways of two parallel strips of wood were laid along the roads. The heavy wheels dug into the wood, so the strips were replaced with iron plates laid by plate layers—a term still used. Train rails are raised above the ground. Train wheels have an inner rim to keep them on the rails.

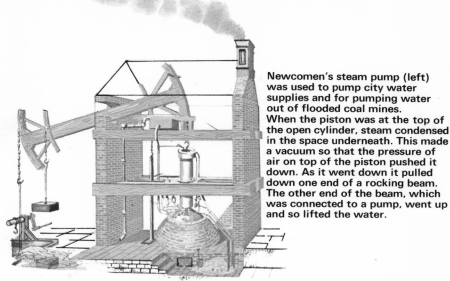

Newcomen's steam pump 1712

Newcomen's steam pump (left) was used to pump city water supplies and for pumping water out of flooded coal mines.
When the piston was at the top of the open cylinder, steam condensed in the space underneath. This made a vacuum so that the pressure of air on top of the piston pushed it down. As it went down it pulled down one end of a rocking beam. The other end of the beam, which was connected to a pump, went up and so lifted the water.

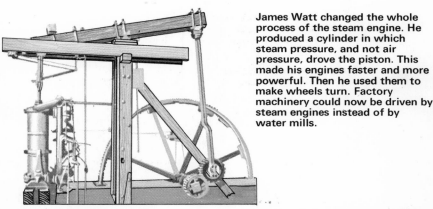

Cugnot's steam tractor 1769

A Frenchman, Cugnot, built a steam tractor (left) in Paris in 1769. It was the first vehicle in the world to go under its own power. It was a gun tractor, for pulling field guns in the French army. The tractor ran out of steam very quickly, so it was never used in battle.

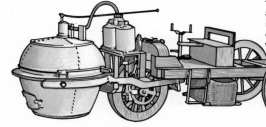

Watt's steam engine 1775

Trevithick's first locomotive 1803

James Watt changed the whole process of the steam engine. He produced a cylinder in which steam pressure, and not air pressure, drove the piston. This made his engines faster and more powerful. Then he used them to make wheels turn. Factory machinery could now be driven by steam engines instead of by water mills.

Richard Trevithick built the first railroad locomotive in the world (below). In 1804 his train carried ten tons of iron and about 70 passengers. The train traveled at about four or five miles an hour.

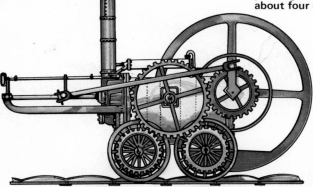
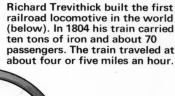

George Stephenson and the first railroads

George Stephenson's engines ran on two cylinders (right). Flames and gases from the fire passed along tubes through the water in the boiler to produce steam. The steam, controlled by a valve, went to the cylinders. Steam on top of the pistons drove them down, and steam below pushed them up again. The up and down movement of the pistons drove connecting rods and cranks, which made the driving wheels go around.

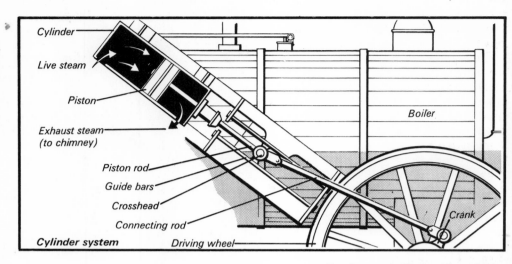

Cylinder

Live steam

Piston

Exhaust steam (to chimney)

Boiler

Piston rod

Guide bars

Crosshead

Connecting rod

Cylinder system

Driving wheel

Crank

Locomotion 1825

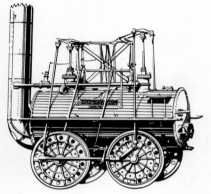

Funnel for water barrel

Water barrel

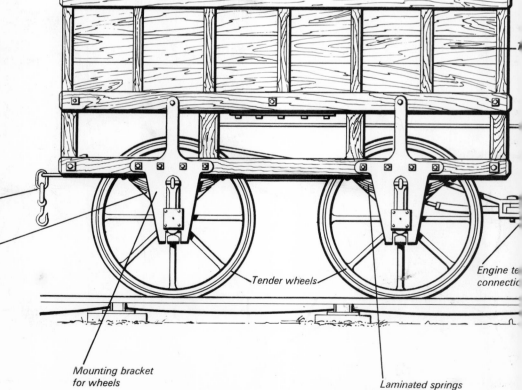

Stephenson built the prize-winning *Rocket* (below) for the Liverpool and Manchester line in 1829. Two important technical improvements helped to make the *Rocket* a success. Steam was raised more quickly by running small fire tubes through the boiler. Stephenson also simplified the driving system by making the pistons and connecting rods work directly onto cranks on the driving wheels. Later, he lowered the heavy cast iron cylinders until they were almost horizontal. This balanced the weight in the engine so that it did not rock so violently from side to side.

The *Locomotion* (above) was George Stephenson's first great engine. At the opening of the Stockton and Darlington railroad in 1825 a horse-rider carrying a Union Jack rode in front of the train. Then Stephenson signaled to him to get out of the way, and the train went faster. It went at 15 to 20mph.

Coupling

Laminated springs

Tender wheels

Engine te connectio

Mounting bracket for wheels

Laminated springs

Industrial railroads

When Trevithick made his first steam locomotive, Britain was in the middle of the Industrial Revolution. Better transport was needed, particularly for the coal and cotton industries. Road transport was slow, and the canal system was also inadequate. Steam-powered railroads solved the problem.

One group of mine-owners wanted to build a railroad to take coal from Darlington to Stockton. At first, the trains were to be horse-drawn. Then an engineer called George Stephenson persuaded the company to give him some money to build a locomotive.

The first public railroad

Stephenson, a miner's son, had started work as a boy in the mines. At nineteen he could not read or write. By the time he built the *Locomotion* for the opening of the Stockton and Darlington line he was an expert engineer. He was to become the 'father of British railroads.'

Stephenson then built the Liverpool and Manchester line, the first full-scale public railroad. He won the prize for the best locomotive with the *Rocket*.

Engine design

Most engines were now following an accepted design. They had a firebox, a boiler with a safety valve in case steam was made too quickly, a smoke-box and a chimney, two cylinders and the wheels. The driest steam rose into the dome above the boiler. From there it went along a main pipe to the cylinders, where valves controlled the amount of steam going in and out. The tender contained coke for the fire, and water for topping up the boiler. A pump fed the water forward.

Stephenson's Rocket 1829

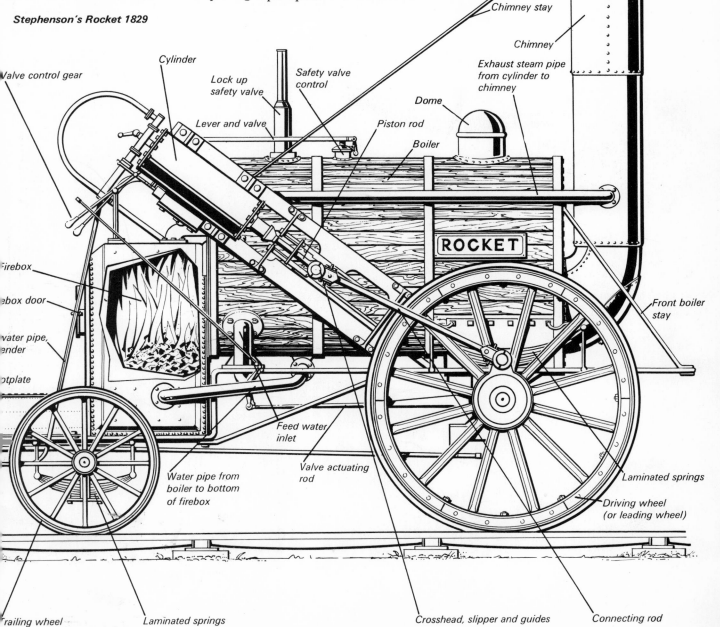

Valve control gear
Cylinder
Lock up safety valve
Safety valve control
Lever and valve
Piston rod
Dome
Boiler
Chimney stay
Chimney
Exhaust steam pipe from cylinder to chimney
Firebox
Firebox door
Water pipe tender
Footplate
Feed water inlet
Water pipe from boiler to bottom of firebox
Valve actuating rod
Front boiler stay
Laminated springs
Driving wheel (or leading wheel)
Trailing wheel
Laminated springs
Crosshead, slipper and guides
Connecting rod

5

Engines and rolling stock before 1850

The London to Birmingham line was finished in 1838. It linked up with the Grand Junction, opened in 1837.
The circular engine sheds (right) on the line into London were called the Roundhouse. They have now been turned into a theater. There were no signal boxes at this time. The switchman (far right) changed the rail points by operating a lever.

Engine sheds near London 1837

Argus 1840

The express engine *Argus* (right) was built to run on rails that were 7ft $\frac{1}{4}$in apart, known as the broad gauge. Stephenson had wanted to make all rails 4ft 8$\frac{1}{2}$in apart.
apart.
Brunel, a famous engineer, laid his London to Bristol, or Great Western line on the broad gauge. This prevented through traffic. Later, a standard gauge rail was added to the broad gauge. The seat on the tender is for the guard.

Typical express engine 1848

The cutaway drawing (right) shows a typical express engine of 1848.
The flat black rod above the connecting rod is part of the mechanism that opens and closes the steam valves. It is called an eccentric.
The main parts are the same as in the *Rocket* of 1829, but the detailed design is more advanced.

Regulator
Fire box
Lever type safety valve
Automatic safety valve
Dome
Chimney
Boiler
Handrail
Foot-plate
Boiler tubes
Blast pipe
Main steam pipe
Eccentric rod
Piston
Connecting rod
Piston rod
Coupling
Feed waterpipe from tender

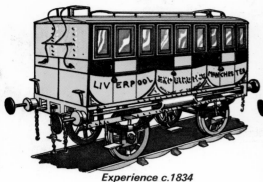

The coach *Experience* (far left) was for first class passengers on the Liverpool to Manchester line. Only one compartment had a light in it. The coach had spring buffers and screw couplings.

A typical third class coach of the same railroad (left) also had spring buffers. Passengers had to stand in open cars. When it rained they stood with their umbrellas up. Seats and roofs were only put on third class coaches in 1844.

Experience c.1834

Typical third class coach 1835

First class coach 1839

First and second class coach 1841

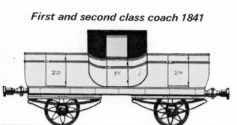

All the compartments of first class coaches (far left) were lit by 1839. By 1841 second class passengers (left) had seats, but no roof. Both coaches ran on the Manchester and Leeds line.

Early freight trains (below) carried anything from cotton and machinery to furniture for moving house. Freight trains now replaced the coal brigs, or boats, delivering coal to London.

Freight train

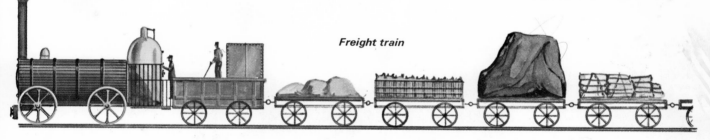

A cauldron with passengers

The first freight cars, or cauldrons (left), were used in mining districts. Later, Trevithick and Stephenson used them to carry passengers in their first trains. The first coaches for third and fourth class passengers were based on these cauldrons. The fares were cheap, but the journey was very uncomfortable.

In the passenger and freight train (below) which ran in 1835, cattle traveled in open cars with men to control them. Third class coaches were usually tacked on to freight trains, much to the passengers' discomfort. There were always long waits at each station while freight cars were shunted off, which also meant the coaches jolted to and fro alarmingly.

Passenger, freight and cattle train 1835

Railroad mania Britain before 1850

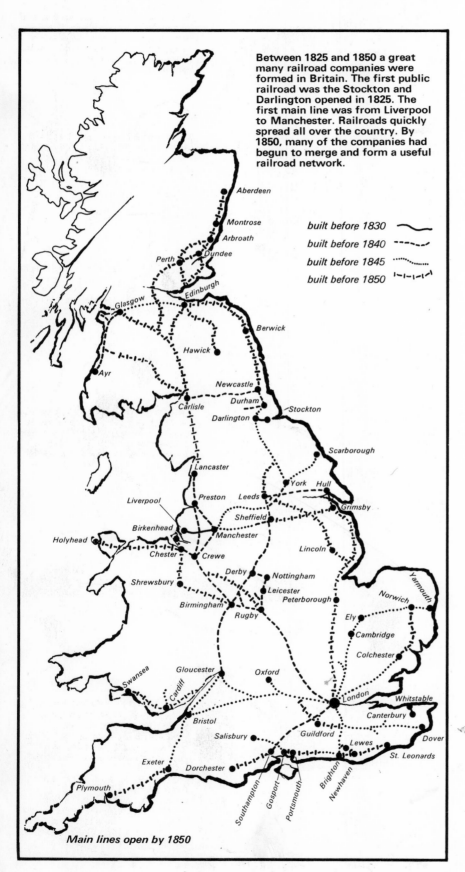

Between 1825 and 1850 a great many railroad companies were formed in Britain. The first public railroad was the Stockton and Darlington opened in 1825. The first main line was from Liverpool to Manchester. Railroads quickly spread all over the country. By 1850, many of the companies had begun to merge and form a useful railroad network.

built before 1830 ——
built before 1840 – – –
built before 1845 ·······
built before 1850 -·-·-·-

Aberdeen
Montrose
Arbroath
Dundee
Perth
Edinburgh
Glasgow
Berwick
Hawick
Ayr
Newcastle
Durham
Carlisle
Stockton
Darlington
Scarborough
Lancaster
York
Hull
Preston
Leeds
Liverpool
Grimsby
Birkenhead
Sheffield
Holyhead
Manchester
Lincoln
Chester
Crewe
Derby
Nottingham
Shrewsbury
Leicester
Peterborough
Yarmouth
Birmingham
Norwich
Rugby
Ely
Cambridge
Colchester
Gloucester
Oxford
Swansea
Cardiff
London
Whitstable
Bristol
Canterbury
Salisbury
Guildford
Dover
Lewes
Exeter
Dorchester
St. Leonards
Southampton
Gosport
Portsmouth
Brighton
Newhaven
Plymouth

Main lines open by 1850

Fortunes won and lost

As soon as the first railroads were under way, many people saw a chance to make their fortune. A group of people would give some money to build a new line, provided they had a share in the profits when the line opened.

In 1845 the 'railroad mania' spread fast. Everyone was trying to make a fortune by investing money in new lines. Many proposals were absurd, and Parliament stopped them. Nevertheless a lot of people went bankrupt.

Food and comfort

Organization and planning were needed. Parliament had already insisted that at least one third class train should run in each direction every day. Passengers now paid a standard fare. Their journey cost them a penny a mile. The coaches had to have seats and roofs, although the sides were still open. Before this, third class passengers had had to stand in open coaches. The 143 mile journey from London to Taunton took 16 hours, which must have been very uncomfortable in bad weather. Passengers traveling from London to Manchester or Liverpool had an even worse time. They had to wait for 15 hours when they changed trains at Birmingham.

After 1846, a great many improvements were made. Even refreshment rooms on the stations were introduced. Most of them were run by the railroad companies themselves. One refreshment room, however, on the Great Western line from London to Bristol, was run by a firm of contractors. To make sure passengers bought food there, the contractors insisted that every train on that line had to make a ten-minute stop at the station.

Dining cars on the train did not yet exist. Nor did sleeping cars or corridor trains. Such comforts were still to come.

Across the Scottish border

In 1846, the chief main lines northwest of London were linked up to form the London and North Western. It was known as the 'Premier Line.' At the same time the first line into Scotland was opened. By 1848 people could travel from London to Carlisle by train.

Rock blasting 1835

Earth removal

The early lines were all built by men using hand tools, horses, and gunpowder for blasting. The line into London (far left) was wide enough to take four lines of rails. The retaining wall on the right held in the earth.

Construction trains carried earth from the cutting (left) for tipping. The earth was built into a high embankment.

Digging the line into London

Digging in the Chiltern Hills

Rock was blasted with gunpowder (far left). The left hand, or down line, is laid on ties. The up line is laid on stone blocks, and may be only a contractor's temporary way.

The men who dug the line through the Chiltern Hills (left) had to be pulled up ramps by a pulley system of ropes. The earth they had cleared from below was dumped at the top.

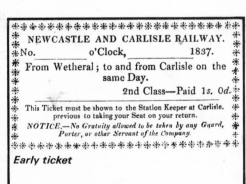

Early ticket

Some early train tickets (above) were made of paper. Each one had to be filled in by hand. Passengers sometimes had to supply such details as their name, age, address, job, where they were going and why.
Cardboard tickets came into use in 1841. They made things much easier. They were simply date-stamped as they were sold.

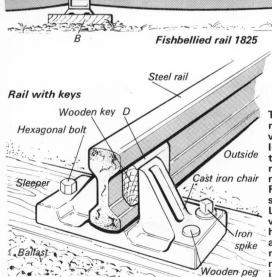

Fishbellied rail 1825

Steel rail

Rail with keys

Wooden key **D**

Hexagonal bolt

Outside

Sleeper

Cast iron chair

Iron spike

Ballast

Wooden peg

The first train rails were iron. The rail (above) sat in chairs (A), which were fixed to ties (B). Iron rails would often bend under the weight of the train. Such rails were known as fishbellied rails.
Fishplates were used to join sections of rail.
Later rails (bottom left) had wooden wedges, or keys (D), to hold the rails in the chairs. From about 1860, iron rails began to be replaced by steel rails. Steel is much tougher and stronger than iron.

9

Railroads spread through Europe

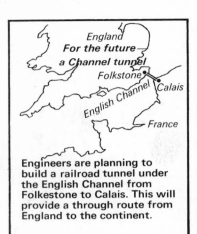

Engineers are planning to build a railroad tunnel under the English Channel from Folkestone to Calais. This will provide a through route from England to the continent.

Every country in Europe began to build a system of railroads. By 1860 France had a very useful network. Prussia, a German state and a great military power, had an even better system.

International expresses were soon running between different capital cities. At one time, only rich people could afford to travel. The railroad soon proved to be much cheaper than traveling by horse-drawn coach, largely because it was so much quicker. It had taken Napoleon two weeks from Paris to Vienna by coach. The same journey by train now took only two days.

The railroads in Europe today stretch out to the ports and frontiers. The gauge in almost every country is standard, at 4ft 8½in. This allows through traffic everywhere except in Russia and Spain, where the gauges are 5ft and 5ft 6in.

Standardization was a great problem when the early railroads began to link up. Not only were there tracks of different width but the loading gauge of the trains themselves had to be within certain limits for through traffic. The loading gauge governs the height and width of a train.

French railroads were strongly influenced by Britain. The train (right) is from Strasbourg to Paris, and ran in the early 1850's. The engine looks very like those built for the Grand Junction railroad in England, but it was probably built in France. The trains also ran on the left hand track, as they did in England.

French train early 1850's

Der Adler 1835

The engine for the first German train (right) was built by Robert Stephenson, George Stephenson's son, in 1835. It was called *Der Adler* (the eagle). The train had one open-sided coach and one with closed compartments.

Austria took the lead in taking a railroad over and through really tough mountain ranges.
The engine of the Austrian express (left) has many British features. The coaches are American in style, especially the wheels and the end doors.

Austrian express 1847

Over the years Spain (below) had been constantly invaded by its neighbor, France. When the railroad age began, Spain decided to protect itself by choosing a different rail gauge from the standard 4ft 8½in gauge used in France. Spain therefore chose a wide gauge of 5ft 6in which meant that no French trains, troop or otherwise, could cross the border. Portugal adopted the same gauge as its neighbor Spain.

Spanish scene mid-1800's

The Alps form a barrier between Italy and Western Europe. A railroad (below) was essential for crossing the mountains at a time when there were no good roads, and of course no air transport. A line was built along the coast from near Cannes, in France, through to Genoa and Rome. The train journey time was shortened several years later when the Mont Cenis tunnel and St. Gotthard route were built. The separate states that made up Italy all accepted the standard gauge. When, in the middle of the 19th century, the states united to become a nation, it already had an efficient railroad system that could take through traffic from other European countries.

Line through the Alps

Engineering miracles early bridges and stations

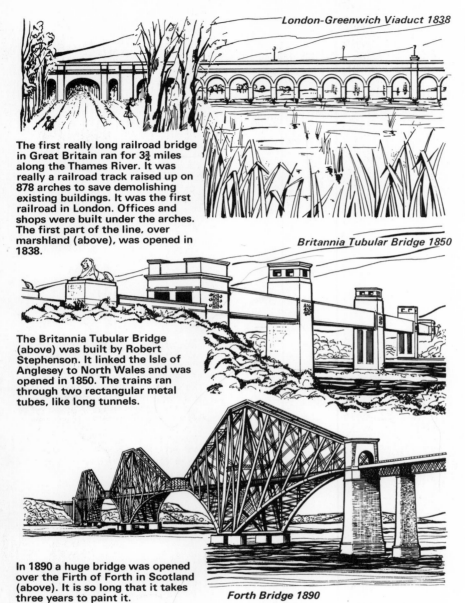

London-Greenwich Viaduct 1838

The first really long railroad bridge in Great Britain ran for 3¾ miles along the Thames River. It was really a railroad track raised up on 878 arches to save demolishing existing buildings. It was the first railroad in London. Offices and shops were built under the arches. The first part of the line, over marshland (above), was opened in 1838.

Britannia Tubular Bridge 1850

The Britannia Tubular Bridge (above) was built by Robert Stephenson. It linked the Isle of Anglesey to North Wales and was opened in 1850. The trains ran through two rectangular metal tubes, like long tunnels.

In 1890 a huge bridge was opened over the Firth of Forth in Scotland (above). It is so long that it takes three years to paint it.

Forth Bridge 1890

Wherever the railroads went, other great works of engineering were performed also. Long tunnels, bridges and magnificent stations were built to serve and improve the rail services.

Famous bridges

In 1879 there was a tragic disaster when the Tay Bridge collapsed while a train was crossing it during a storm. So when the great Forth Bridge was built, the engineers took many safety precautions. Models were built to test the strength of the bridge under all weather conditions and under heavy loads. It is the longest cantilever bridge in Britain.

The biggest cantilever span in the world is 1,800ft long on the Quebec Bridge over the St. Lawrence River in Canada. The scheme was begun in 1899 and the present bridge took 18 years to build.

Underground railroads

The problem of providing rail transport in large, built-up cities, such as Paris, London and New York, was solved by building subways. The first one, for steam trains, was built in London. The streets were so congested with horse drawn traffic that it was difficult to cross the town. The first subway was built by simply digging up the streets, digging a trench for the rails and re-covering it.

By 1882 the completely underground Circle Line was built in London. It became fashionable to buy a return ticket and just ride around the Circle Line to see what it was like.

Royal Albert Bridge 1859

The Royal Albert Bridge (right), was opened by Prince Albert, Queen Victoria's husband, in 1859. It was built by the famous engineer Isambard Brunel, who had built the Great Western broad gauge railroad. The bridge, which ran across the Tamar River in south-west England, had only one line of broad gauge rails.
Brunel was French by birth, but he lived and worked in England and became a British subject. He built some famous ships as well as railroads and bridges, and was very wealthy. He died soon after the Royal Albert Bridge was opened.

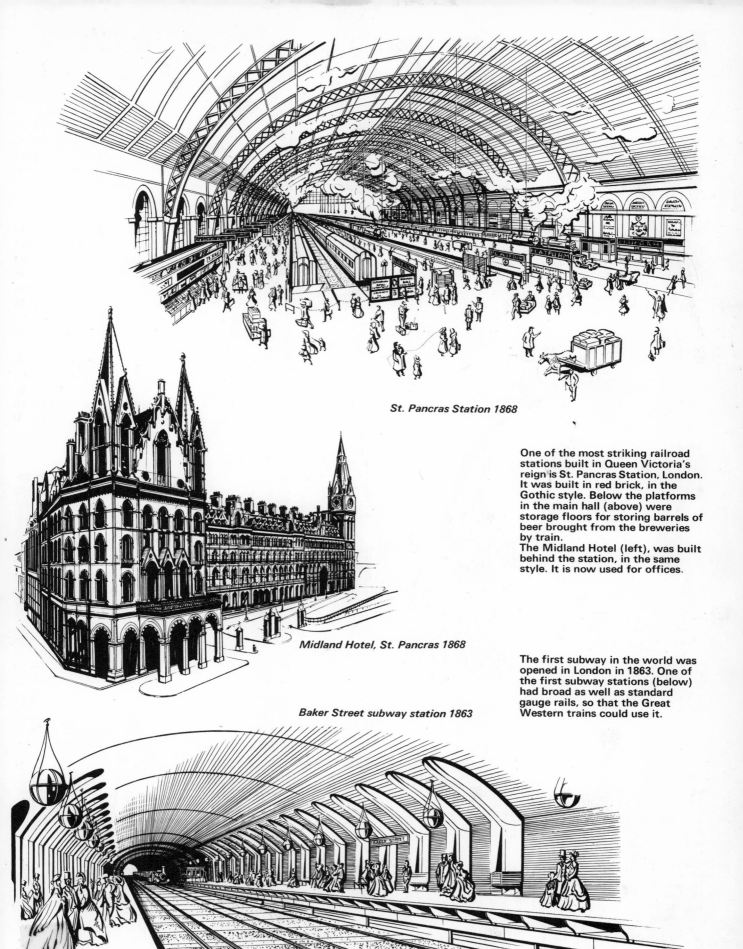

St. Pancras Station 1868

Midland Hotel, St. Pancras 1868

One of the most striking railroad stations built in Queen Victoria's reign is St. Pancras Station, London. It was built in red brick, in the Gothic style. Below the platforms in the main hall (above) were storage floors for storing barrels of beer brought from the breweries by train.

The Midland Hotel (left), was built behind the station, in the same style. It is now used for offices.

Baker Street subway station 1863

The first subway in the world was opened in London in 1863. One of the first subway stations (below) had broad as well as standard gauge rails, so that the Great Western trains could use it.

Early American trains

Railroads in Carolina

An entirely steam-operated railroad was opened in North America in South Carolina in 1830. It had a 5ft gauge, which became usual in the South until after the Civil War of 1861–65. The flood of railroads in the North largely adopted the standard 4ft 8½in gauge.

At first, some of these northern lines bought engines from England. The British-built locomotive *Stourbridge Lion* ran on test on the Delaware and Hudson line in 1829. American manufacturers soon began to produce their own high quality machinery and passenger and freight vehicles.

In America, iron was difficult to obtain and the rails were not very strong. To give more support, cheap wooden ties, called sleepers in Britain, were laid very close together.

Transcontinental line

By 1835 half of the world's railroads were in the United States and as they pushed inland from the East Coast the idea of a transcontinental line was born. It was opened from East to West in 1869, four years after the end of the Civil War.

A short section of the South Carolina railroad was opened only three months after the English Liverpool and Manchester line. It was the second railroad in the world to be worked entirely by steam. By 1833 it was 136 miles long, and far longer than any other railroad yet built.
The engine of the first train (right) was called *The Best Friend of Charleston.* It was built in New York. The vertical boiler was wood-fired and the two barrels in the tender probably contained feed water. In the two carriages with their wagonette-type bodies the seats were back to back. There were canvas side and end screens which could be lowered in bad weather.

First train on the South Carolina Railroad 1830

The Mohawk and Hudson Railroad was opened in 1831 (right). Unlike *The Best Friend of Charleston,* the engine had a horizontal boiler. It was called *De Witt Clinton.* But it broke down, and the second train had to be drawn by horses.
The carriages look like ordinary road coaches mounted on railroad wheels. This type of vehicle did not last long in the United States. The rails were laid on massive stone blocks.

Opening of the Mohawk and Hudson Railroad 1831

In winter a huge headlamp was necessary to light up large obstacles like snow-laden trees, which often fell across the line. Sometimes the light track broke up, either from severe frost or floods or from the weight of an earlier train. Forest fires were another hazard. The cowcatcher swept away smaller obstacles, such as animals that strayed on to the tracks.

There is much decorative work on the engine (left), but, as on most American engines, there are no splashers—or mudguards—over the coupled wheels. In bad weather the wheels would get wet and spin on steep or poor rails, so the rails had to be sanded to give the wheels a better grip.

Typical American engine 1860

Engine on the Chicago and North Western Railroad 1855

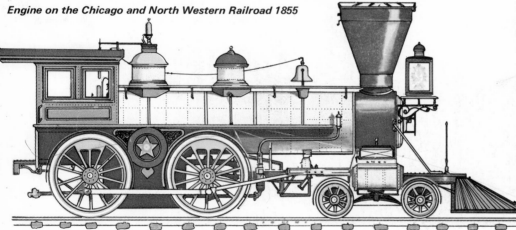

By the early 1850's development of American engines had grown. The first tracks were often laid quickly and roughly. To make the ride smoother, a small four-wheeled, pivoted front unit was added to the engine. It was called a bogie, and it guided the front of the engine very well. Because of its good riding it was also used for tenders and passenger and freight cars. Even longer and better passenger vehicles could be drawn by two bogies. The engine (left), which belonged to the Chicago and North Western Railroad is a well-finished American engine. The cowcatcher, headlamp and large cab for the crew were a few of the improvements.

Bridge on the Washington to Virginia line 1860's

The American Civil War, from 1861 to 1865, affected American railroads. Vast armies were employed and for the first time troops could be assembled quickly by rail. Supplies of all kinds were conveyed to appropriate rail heads, and in places there was much raiding and fighting to destroy the railroads and their depots.

One bridge (left) which was raided and wrecked was on the line from Washington into Virginia. Military engineers repaired it temporarily.

Conquest of the Alps

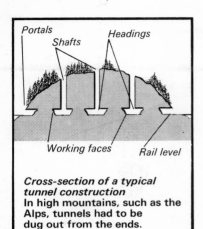

Cross-section of a typical tunnel construction
In high mountains, such as the Alps, tunnels had to be dug out from the ends.

Labels in diagram: Portals, Shafts, Headings, Working faces, Rail level

Railroads in Switzerland

There are three principal types of railroads in Switzerland: standard gauge, meter gauge and narrow gauge lines. The standard gauge lines make up the bulk of the system. The narrow gauge scenic mountain railroads climb very steeply; some of them are closed in winter.

At the turn of the century the Swiss Government nationalized the majority of the railroads. Electrification was begun in 1919. Hydroelectric schemes generated the power from mountain torrents.

The great tunnels

The first Alpine tunnel, the Mont Cenis, was $8\frac{1}{4}$ miles long. It gave a direct route from Paris to Turin. There were no modern explosives or equipment then, so it took 13 years to build. A temporary mountain railroad was laid over the pass. This was wrecked by avalanches and had to be repaired.

The north-south route across Switzerland is the St. Gotthard line, taking traffic through the St. Gotthard tunnel. It is $9\frac{1}{4}$ miles long. It took nine years to dig and cost many lives. There are 79 tunnels and 324 bridges on the line.

The map (right) shows the principal Swiss railroads, the locations of the great Alpine tunnels and the international connecting routes.

The first railroad to be built over a mountain range in Europe was at Semmering, in Austria. It was opened in 1854.

Route map of Switzerland showing the great tunnels

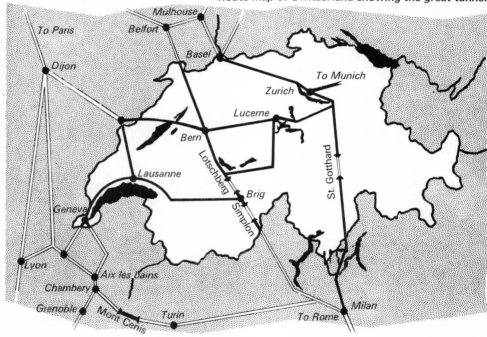

The Simplon Tunnel (right) was built to improve the route from Paris to Milan. It runs from Brig, in Switzerland to Iselle, in Italy. It is over $12\frac{1}{4}$ miles long, the longest main line tunnel in the world. Originally it was only a single line of track with a passing place in the middle. Later it was doubled. The first half of the tunnel was opened in 1906 after it had taken seven years to build. The hydraulic drill had hollow cutters which wore down from two feet to three inches. On some days 300 cutters were used up. The construction of the great tunnels was a tremendous achievement. Ventilation, blasting fumes, flooding and crumbling rock were major problems.

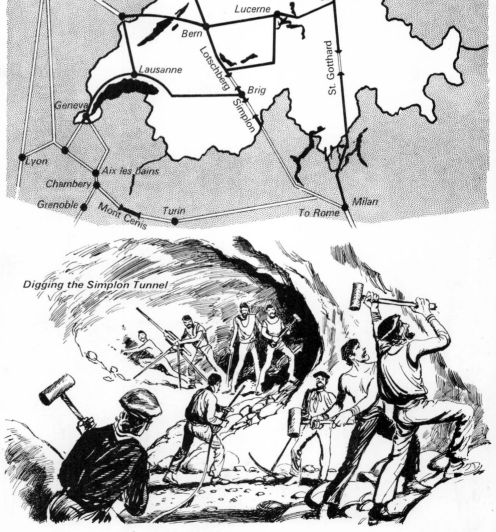

Digging the Simplon Tunnel

Express on the St. Gotthard line

An express train with a powerful four-cylinder compound engine (left) in a scenic setting on the St Gotthard line. The 4-6-0 locomotive was built in the middle of the 1890's. It has automatic air brakes. These work by compressed air and act on every wheel along the train. The compressed air reservoir is the long cylindrical tank above the driving and trailing coupled wheels.

The spiral layout of the St. Gotthard line

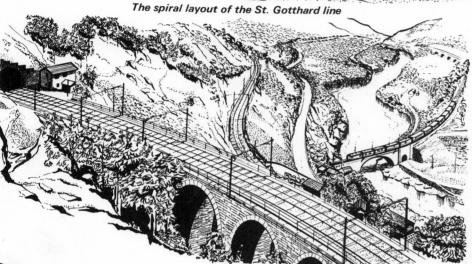

There are several ways of gaining or losing height in restricted valleys or on the sides of mountains. One of these is to use spiral tunnels to ease the grade. The entrances are above or below one another.
The St. Gotthard main line (left) is on three levels. The train is about to enter the spiral Travi tunnel, and the tunnel in the foreground is the Piano Tondo.

The Landwasser viaduct

The Landwasser viaduct (left) is supported on five high columns rising up from the valley floor. It is on the Rhaetian meter gauge railroad which links Chur to St. Moritz in Switzerland. Some of these smaller lines are closed in winter.

Development of the locomotive 1850—1890

Tank engine 1852

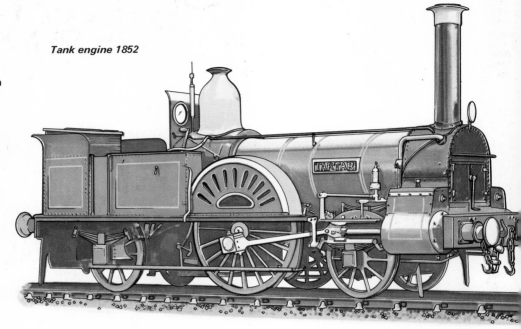

The *Tartar* tank engine (right) is a 2-2-2 WT (well tank) engine from the London and South Western Railway. Instead of carrying the water tanks along either side of the boiler, the WT type of tank engine has a single tank beneath the footplate and coal bunker, forming a well.

The London and South Western Railway 2-2-2 *Victoria* (right) was built in 1859, but the cab was added later. The driving wheel is 6ft 6in in diameter. The original color of the paintwork was brick red but this was changed later to dark brown. The *Victoria* was the last 'single' to be built for this railroad, and it was the last of this type to survive. It was sold in 1885.

Express engine 1859

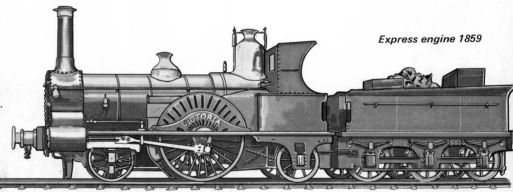

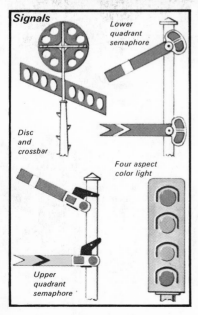

Signals

Lower quadrant semaphore

Disc and crossbar

Four aspect color light

Upper quadrant semaphore

Changes in design

By 1850, designers were beginning to take great pride in the appearance of their engines, as well as in technical progress. At this stage, Britain was still leading the rest of Europe in engine design, and exporting to many countries. All the major advances in design can be seen in British-built models.

Technical advances were largely concerned with speed and power. It was more practical to have one standard engine design for both passenger and freight trains. But the 'single' engine type was best for passenger trains, while engines with small coupled wheels were best for hauling freight. Speed depends largely on the diameter of the driving wheels. The 'single' engine type had a single, large, driving wheel rising on each side of the boiler. This limited the diameter of the boiler. The problem was solved by increasing the pressure of the steam without increasing the size of the boiler. (At a higher pressure, less steam is needed for each stroke of the double pistons which turn the driving wheels.)

The problem of adhesion

An increase in engine power caused an adhesion problem. If the power was too great, the driving, or coupled, wheels would lose their grip on the rails and simply spin around freely. If, however, the weight on the axles was increased to prevent this spinning, the rails might not be strong enough to take the extra weight. In the latter half of the century strong steel rails replaced the existing iron ones, which solved this problem.

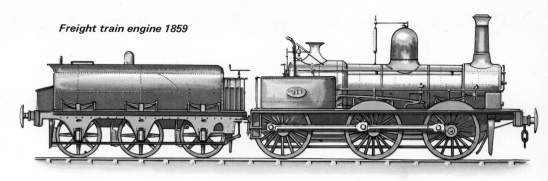

Freight train engine 1859

The dark olive-green freight train engine (right) on the London, Brighton and South Coast Railway has a neat but stark design. It is remarkable because of the height of its dome. The 4ft 9in diameter coupled wheels were originally secondhand cast iron ones, but these were replaced with the standard pattern.

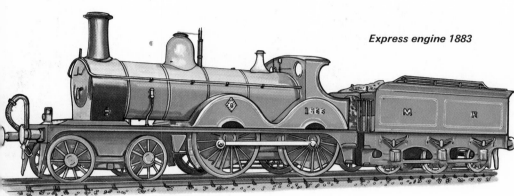

Express engine 1883

The design of the Midland Railway 4-4-0 No. 1666 express (left), is well proportioned, neat and symmetrical. This class of engine was fast and ran very smoothly although the boiler was not large. It was built at Derby in 1883.

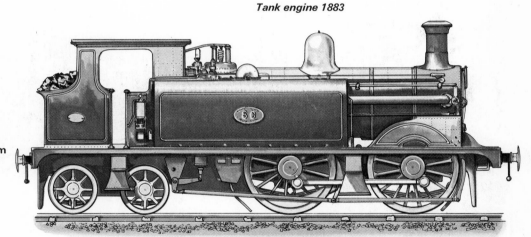

Tank engine 1883

Robert Stephenson built the London, Chatham and Dover Railway tank engine 0-4-4 No. 80 (right) in 1883. The engine was fitted with gear for turning the exhaust steam back into water. This was to prevent the tunnels filling with steam on the London subway lines.

The large horizontal pipe from the smokebox takes exhaust steam into the side tank where it is condensed.

Freight train engine 1887

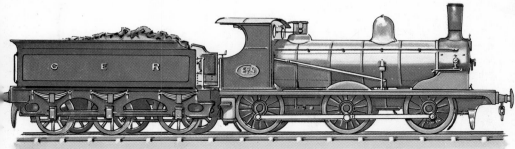

The Stratford-built freight train engine of 1887 (left) originally had 4ft 10in coupled wheels, but this was later increased one inch by fitting thicker tires.

This was an extremely successful engine design. It remained the standard Great Eastern freight train engine from 1883 until the end of the century and 289 engines were built to this pattern. They could go almost anywhere and they provide a good example of successful standardization.

Victorian locomotives and stock

Stirling Single No. 1 1870

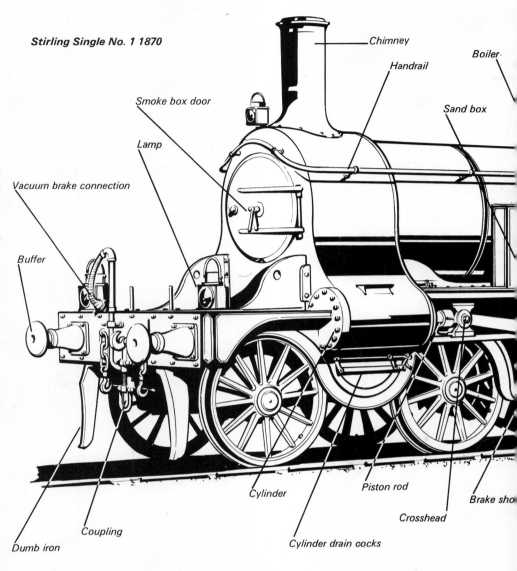

One of the finest express engines of the mid-Victorian era was the *Stirling Single No. 1* (right). It was built by Patrick Stirling in 1870 and has now been preserved. Stirling engines hauled the *Flying Scotsman* express.

The Stirling engine is classed as a 4-2-2. These numbers always apply to the number of wheels of each type that an engine has. The first number is the number of wheels on the front bogie or 'pony truck.' The second is the total number of driving wheels. The third number indicates how many trailing wheels there are under the fire box. The Stirling is called a 'single' because it has a single driving wheel on each side.

In some engines, the coal and water were carried in a tender. An engine without a tender is called a tank engine. The water is carried in tanks on the engine, and coal in a bunker behind the footplate.

The cutaway drawing (right) shows the first British train coach to have a side corridor. It was built by the Great Northern Railway in 1882.

At each end was a lavatory, one for ladies and one for gentlemen.

There were no connecting doors to other carriages.

Chimney

Handrail

Boiler

Sand box

Smoke box door

Lamp

Vacuum brake connection

Buffer

Dumb iron

Coupling

Cylinder

Cylinder drain cocks

Piston rod

Crosshead

Brake sho

Great Northern Railway third class coach 1877

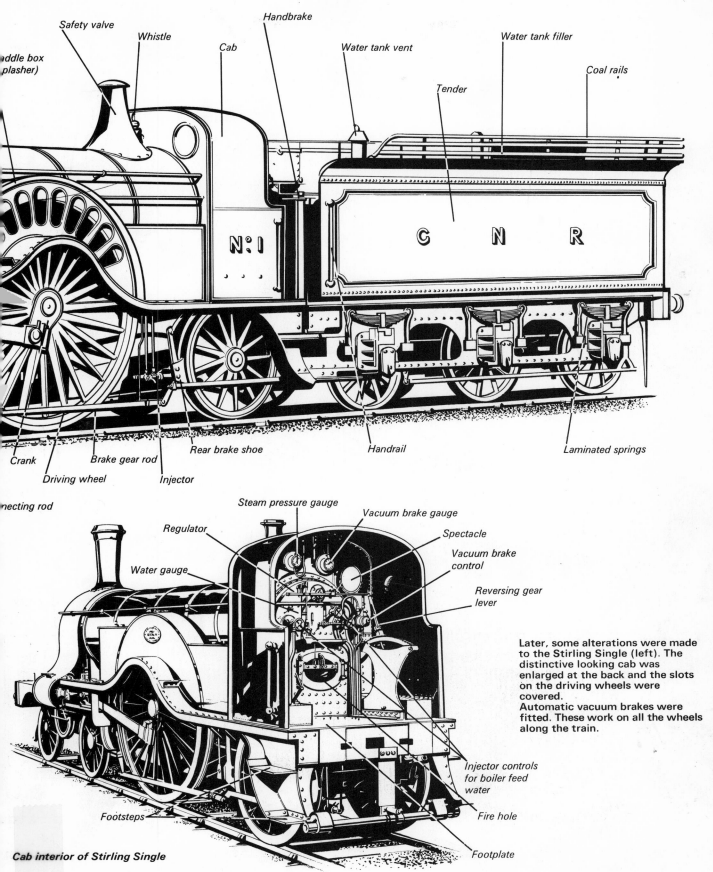

Safety valve

Whistle

Handbrake

Cab

Water tank vent

Water tank filler

Coal rails

Tender

(addle box
plasher)

C N R

N° I

Crank

Brake gear rod

Rear brake shoe

Handrail

Laminated springs

Driving wheel

Injector

necting rod

Steam pressure gauge

Vacuum brake gauge

Regulator

Spectacle

Water gauge

Vacuum brake
control

Reversing gear
lever

Later, some alterations were made
to the Stirling Single (left). The
distinctive looking cab was
enlarged at the back and the slots
on the driving wheels were
covered.
Automatic vacuum brakes were
fitted. These work on all the wheels
along the train.

Injector controls
for boiler feed
water

Footsteps

Fire hole

Footplate

Cab interior of Stirling Single

First transcontinental railroads in America

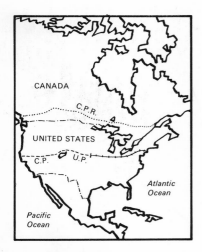

Map of North America shows the first transcontinental railroads; the Canadian Pacific (C.P.R.) in Canada and the Union Pacific (U.P.) linked to the Central Pacific (C.P.).

When the United States took California from Mexico in 1846, travel overland was very difficult. The practical solution was to build a railroad and the projected line was started westwards from St. Louis in 1851, but it did not get beyond Kansas City.

Then in 1862-63 two lines were begun, the Central Pacific from San Francisco, in the west, and the Union Pacific from Omaha in Nebraska which was already linked with the Atlantic by rail. The Rocky Mountains were difficult and in many points along the route military guards had to be provided to protect the workmen from Indians. Construction was also delayed by the Civil War. The two approaching lines were eventually joined in 1869. The first transcontinental railroad was completed: more were to follow very soon.

Canadian Pacific

Meanwhile, Canada had decided to follow suit. It then took five months to cross from Montreal to Vancouver in the summer, but on the opening of the Canadian Pacific Railway in 1885, the journey took five days. Unlike the American lines it formed one continuous system from the St. Lawrence to the Pacific.

Central Pacific Locomotive 1867

By 1867 the Union Pacific was 500 miles west of the Missouri River. The locomotive (right) in one of the many camps and equipment depots, is typical of the period. By this time the Central Pacific went over the rocky Sierras; the summit height was over 8,000ft. The track descended to the Utah desert where the contestants met. The line ran from Omaha to San Francisco, a distance of 1,770 miles.

The completion of America's first transcontinental route, 1869

The Central Pacific and the Union Pacific lines were supposed to meet in Utah. The rival companies, however, refused to join up and the two tracks were built side by side for 225 miles before they agreed to link up. The occasion was marked by two trains slowly moving up the two sections of track to face each other at the junction (right).

The Canadian Pacific Railway was a tremendous feat of engineering. It included 2,500 miles of new line, and many bridges and tunnels.

Wood was used for the construction of bridges and also as fuel. A freight train (left) is crossing a very high wooden trestle bridge. The train's high chimney is to prevent sparks flying from the wood-fired engine and setting fire to the bridges and forests.

Canadian Pacific freight train

Coal-fired Union Pacific freight train 1885

A Union Pacific freight train (left) of about 1885 had a small-wheeled 4-4-0 engine and a small boiler, but big cylinders. The engine was coal-fired, and therefore had no spark-arresting chimney.

Before long engines for this type of train became much larger.

The Great Salt Lake bridge

When the Union Pacific was first built, the track ran around the edge of the Great Salt Lake in Utah. Later on, a long trestle bridge and embankments, 31½ miles long, were built across the lake. This made the journey much shorter. The large passenger train (left) is on this lake crossing, which has a double track. More double track sections and more powerful engines were introduced to speed up the journey.

Railroads under attack armored trains

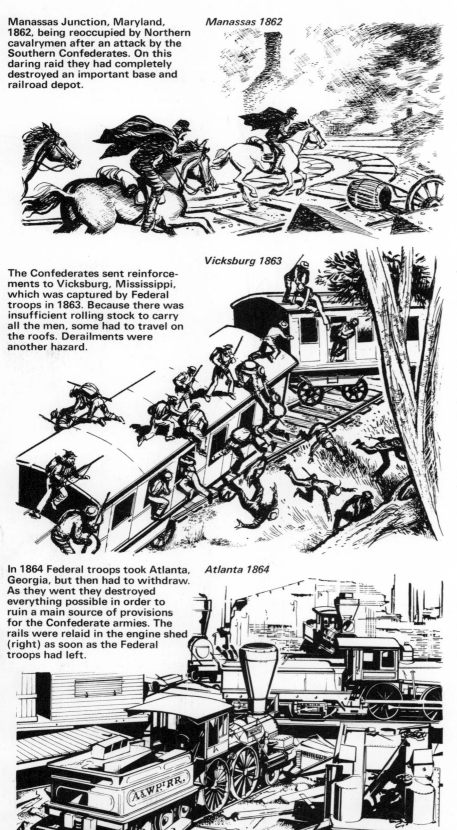

Manassas Junction, Maryland, 1862, being reoccupied by Northern cavalrymen after an attack by the Southern Confederates. On this daring raid they had completely destroyed an important base and railroad depot.

Manassas 1862

The Confederates sent reinforcements to Vicksburg, Mississippi, which was captured by Federal troops in 1863. Because there was insufficient rolling stock to carry all the men, some had to travel on the roofs. Derailments were another hazard.

Vicksburg 1863

In 1864 Federal troops took Atlanta, Georgia, but then had to withdraw. As they went they destroyed everything possible in order to ruin a main source of provisions for the Confederate armies. The rails were relaid in the engine shed (right) as soon as the Federal troops had left.

Atlanta 1864

Railroads in occupied territories

Perhaps the earliest use of railroads in war was towards the end of the Crimean campaign in 1855. A line was laid along the quays of the British base port of Balaclava and a short distance inland. It was a purely military railroad and was dismantled later.

The railroads played a prominent part in the American Civil War (1861–65). The existing lines were used by each side for transporting troops, and also as the targets of raids to hamper the movements of the opposing forces. Strategic points changed hands several times being taken alternately by the Federal troops (from the North) and the Confederates (from the South).

In 1866, Prussia, who had built her railroads with a strategic aim, was able to concentrate her troops rapidly. She outmaneuvered and defeated Austria who had laid out her railroads on a commercial pattern. Then, in 1870–71, Prussia defeated France by the same methods. Armies became amazingly mobile. In addition, railroads could be used for actual fighting. Armored trains were invented. They were a new threat to unshielded opponents but they could be wrecked by removing a fishplate or rail, or by mining the track.

The British campaign in the Sudan, which ended in 1898, was based entirely on a military railroad from the Red Sea. It was built to the same 3ft 6in gauge as the South African lines, since it was hoped that they would join up one day.

Armored trains

The first armored train ever used was converted from an ordinary train and used in Egypt in 1882. The idea was soon copied by many nations.

In the Boer War in South Africa (1899-1902) railroads played a most important part as far as the British were concerned. Armored trains were used to defend the lines from enemy attack. These trains were built in Cape Town. They were unbearably hot in summer since there were no ventilation or cooling slats in either the heavily armored fighting vehicles or the engine.

Armored trains and rail mounted guns were built in Britain for coastal defense in case of invasion, but they were never used.

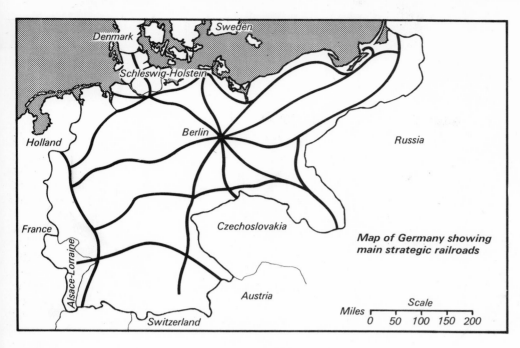

Map of Germany showing main strategic railroads

In 1861, led by von Bismarck, the Prussians began to build up their forces and plan a railroad system for use in the war, that was to give them the leadership of the German Confederation.

The map (left) shows how the main lines radiated from the center at Berlin, to well sited arsenals and fortresses and onward to the frontiers and coasts. In the interior there were lines which gave easy movement to right and left.

The armored gun truck (below) was built for a Sussex coast defense unit before World War I. The weapon is a naval type 40-pounder, and the armored turret can be turned through an angle of 360°.

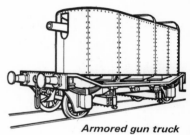

Armored gun truck

The first improvised armored train 1882

The first armored train (left) was an ingenious conversion made by two naval officers. They mounted a 40-pounder naval gun and some light machine guns in front of some freight cars, armoring it with sheet steel plates. The engine was protected by hanging sandbags around the boiler. It was used during a military operation to restore order in Egypt in 1882.

The armored train (below) was used by the British in the Boer War of 1899–1902. It was built in Cape Town and was used to keep the line open from Belmont to the Modder.

South African armored train

25

Trains across the World

The 19th century Indian express (right) is typical of the stock used at the time. The Indian rail network, begun in 1852, was carefully planned in advance, and built in stages. It became one of the best in the British Empire. There were six principal systems on the 5ft 6in gauge, a meter gauge system of local lines and some narrow gauge mountain railroads.

Indian Midland Railway express

Sydney-Bendigo train, Australia

The Sydney-Bendigo train (right) at the turn of the century. The first railroad in Australia was the Melbourne suburban line, begun in 1854. Here and all over the State of Victoria, the Irish gauge of 5ft 3in was used. The same gauge was used in South Australia. Railroads in other parts of the country were built independently, on different gauges. In 1917, the last section of the first trans-continental link was built to the standard gauge. It ran between South and Western Australia.

The two islands of New Zealand have two separate rail systems, but they are part of one organization. Both islands have very mountainous country, and both use the 3ft 6in gauge. There are some magnificent tunnels and bridges. The steep gradients slow the trains down but communications are good.

The popular *Geyserland Express* on North Island (right) runs from Auckland to Rotorura. It takes many tourists to see the spectacular geysers in the region.

Geyserland Express, New Zealand

Imperial Limited, Canada

In 1900, one of the most famous trains was the *Imperial Limited* (left) of the Canadian Pacific. It took five days to cover the 3,000 miles from Montreal to Vancouver. Before the railroad was built it took five months to cross Canada.

Johannesburg-Cape Town express, South Africa

The South African Railways began in 1859. There were two main lines, one from Cape Town to Kimberley, the other from Port Elizabeth to Johannesburg and Pretoria. The railroads developed rapidly with the Kimberley diamond rush and also served the Witwatersrand goldfields which opened in 1886. The Johannesburg-Cape Town Express (left) is now run by the integrated South African Railways and Harbours system.

Mail trains, Rhodesia

The Rhodesian Railways were originally intended to be a part of a fantastic scheme to have a line right down Africa from north to south—the Cape to Cairo Railway.

The two mail trains (left) are on a passing loop on a single main line.

One of the most magnificent views from a train in Rhodesia is of the Victoria Falls which are spanned by a bridge 420ft high with a single line track.

Royal trains carriages fit for a king

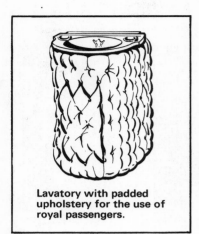

Lavatory with padded upholstery for the use of royal passengers.

Queen Victoria traveled by train for the first time in 1842. From then on the Royal Family traveled by train whenever possible, but the Queen did not like speed and objected to going at more than 40mph.

Special safety precautions were taken for royal trains. All movements on the line were stopped by a pilot engine which ran a quarter of an hour ahead of the royal train. Points were padlocked, watchmen were posted at all crossings, bridges and stations, platelayers patrolled the line and special precautions were taken with signaling.

In Britain, Royalty pay their fares just like other passengers. They also pay for the use of the special trains that have been built for them by the railroad companies. The Royal Family are always consulted about the furnishings for the interior. King Edward VII said 'Make it like a yacht.' There were also train coaches kept at Calais for British royalty traveling abroad. King George V had to spend so much time on the train during the 1914–18 war that he had baths installed.

One of the most elaborate royal trains was built for Maximilian II of Bavaria.

In 1842 the London and Birmingham railroad built a special train coach (right) for Queen Adelaide, the widow of King William IV. It was four-wheeled with two compartments and an anteroom for attendants. Rail travel was not very comfortable in the early days, even for a queen. On Queen Adelaide's train there was no heating, only footwarmers. There were only two oil lamps. There were no brakes on the coach, but it did have spring buffers and gold-plated handrails and door-handles.

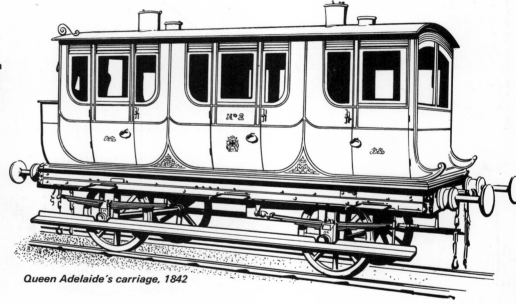

Queen Adelaide's carriage, 1842

When King Louis Philippe of France was on a State Visit to Britain a Pullman car was used for the royal reception (right) at the station at Gosport, where he was greeted by Queen Victoria and Prince Albert. At the request of his government the King never traveled by train in France. They were concerned for his safety after there had been a severe rail accident at Meudon, near Paris.

Royal reception at Gosport station

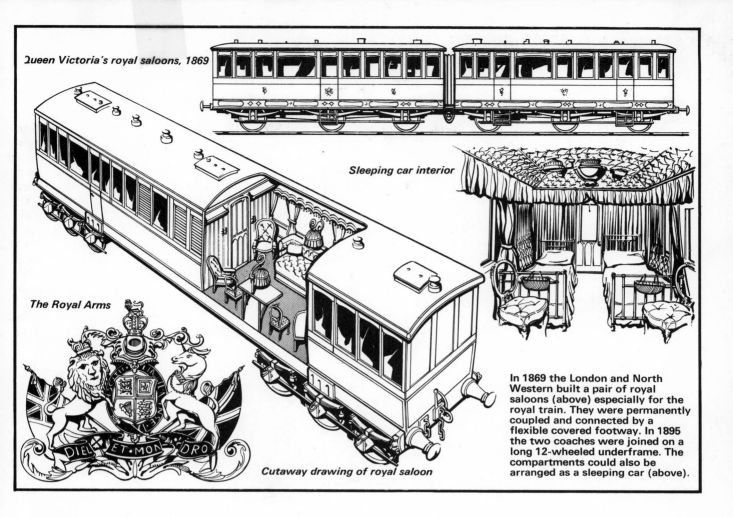

Queen Victoria's royal saloons, 1869

Sleeping car interior

The Royal Arms

DIEU · ET · MON · DROIT

Cutaway drawing of royal saloon

In 1869 the London and North Western built a pair of royal saloons (above) especially for the royal train. They were permanently coupled and connected by a flexible covered footway. In 1895 the two coaches were joined on a long 12-wheeled underframe. The compartments could also be arranged as a sleeping car (above).

The Queen, 1897

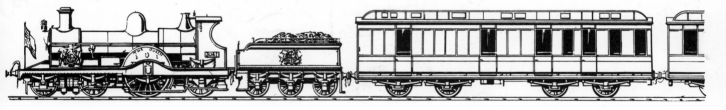

Queen Victoria traveled by train (above) from Windsor to London on the occasion of her Diamond Jubilee in 1897. The engine is one of the Great Western 'singles,' *The Queen,* especially decorated and flying the Royal Standard.

The Khedive of Egypt's engine, 1859

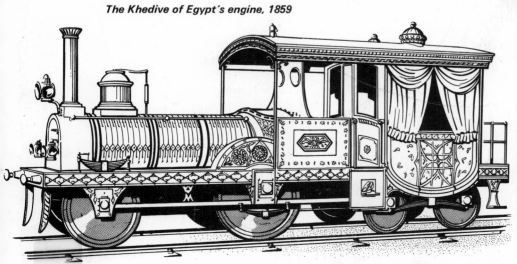

This early steam engine (left) was built for the Khedive of Egypt in 1859 by Robert Stephenson. The engine and passenger compartment are all on the same frame. It was built to the standard gauge and ran on the Egyptian State Railways. It was lavishly and expensively decorated, but although the line was unfenced there was no cowcatcher.

Golden age of railroads

Rail networks expand

By the turn of the century the expanding rail systems linked towns and villages that had previously had very poor communications. In England the plan was to have few villages more than 12 miles away from a railroad station to which horse-drawn carriages took traffic. Later, buses came into use, first to feed, but later to compete with, the railroads.

International expresses

Main line services were constantly improving and on the continent many national and international express services were introduced. The coaches were well furnished and belonged to a company with the grand name of *Compagnie Internationale des Wagons-Lits et des Grands Express Européens*. They could be seen everywhere, from France to China. Passengers could travel straight across two continents by train.

Pullman trains

In America, George Pullman started the luxurious Pullman service. In his 'hotel cars' passengers could eat, sleep and ride in great comfort.

In 1908 the London, Brighton and South Coast Railway introduced a Pullman Car express to run between London and Brighton. It was to be non-stop for the hour's run, which was good timing since it could not really speed up until it was clear of the London suburbs. On this service the company often used large 'Atlantic' type engines. One of the second series hauls the *Southern Belle* express (right).

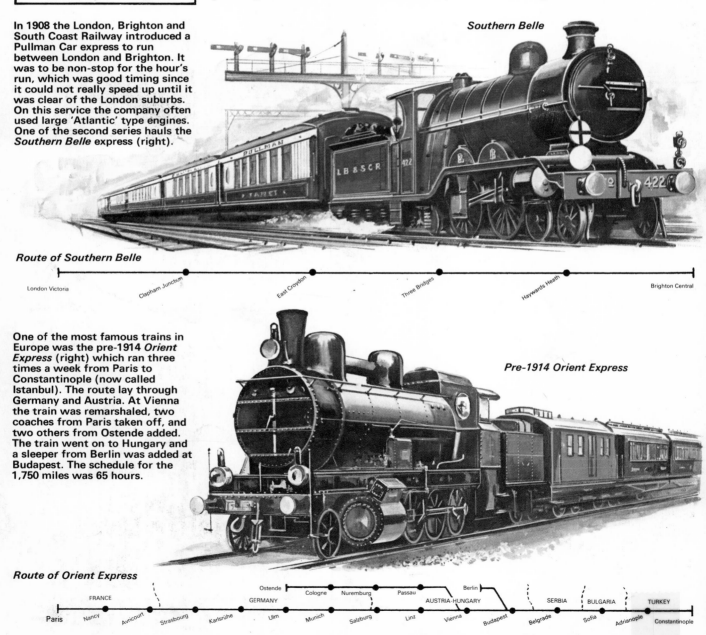

Southern Belle

Route of Southern Belle

London Victoria — Clapham Junction — East Croydon — Three Bridges — Haywards Heath — Brighton Central

One of the most famous trains in Europe was the pre-1914 *Orient Express* (right) which ran three times a week from Paris to Constantinople (now called Istanbul). The route lay through Germany and Austria. At Vienna the train was remarshaled, two coaches from Paris taken off, and two others from Ostende added. The train went on to Hungary and a sleeper from Berlin was added at Budapest. The schedule for the 1,750 miles was 65 hours.

Pre-1914 Orient Express

Route of Orient Express

FRANCE · Ostende · Cologne · Nuremburg · Passau · Berlin · GERMANY · AUSTRIA-HUNGARY · SERBIA · BULGARIA · TURKEY

Paris · Nancy · Avricourt · Strasbourg · Karlsrühe · Ulm · Munich · Salzburg · Linz · Vienna · Budapest · Belgrade · Sofia · Adrianople · Constantinople

Twentieth Century Limited

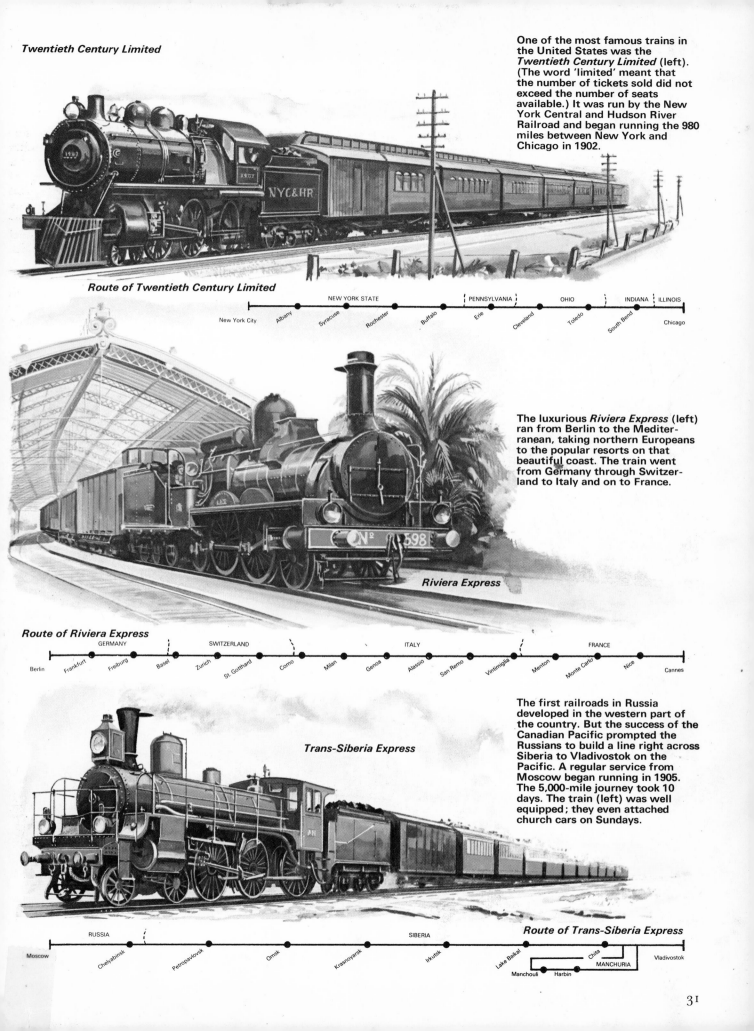

One of the most famous trains in the United States was the *Twentieth Century Limited* (left). (The word 'limited' meant that the number of tickets sold did not exceed the number of seats available.) It was run by the New York Central and Hudson River Railroad and began running the 980 miles between New York and Chicago in 1902.

Route of Twentieth Century Limited

NEW YORK STATE — PENNSYLVANIA — OHIO — INDIANA — ILLINOIS

New York City · Albany · Syracuse · Rochester · Buffalo · Erie · Cleveland · Toledo · South Bend · Chicago

The luxurious *Riviera Express* (left) ran from Berlin to the Mediterranean, taking northern Europeans to the popular resorts on that beautiful coast. The train went from Germany through Switzerland to Italy and on to France.

Riviera Express

Route of Riviera Express

GERMANY — SWITZERLAND — ITALY — FRANCE

Berlin · Frankfurt · Freiburg · Basel · Zurich · St. Gotthard · Como · Milan · Genoa · Alassio · San Remo · Vintimiglia · Menton · Monte Carlo · Nice · Cannes

Trans-Siberia Express

The first railroads in Russia developed in the western part of the country. But the success of the Canadian Pacific prompted the Russians to build a line right across Siberia to Vladivostok on the Pacific. A regular service from Moscow began running in 1905. The 5,000-mile journey took 10 days. The train (left) was well equipped; they even attached church cars on Sundays.

Route of Trans-Siberia Express

RUSSIA — SIBERIA — MANCHURIA

Moscow · Chelyabinsk · Petropavlovsk · Omsk · Krasnoyarsk · Irkutsk · Lake Baikal · Manchouli · Harbin · Chita · Vladivostok

31

Trains and two World Wars

Germany's well planned railroads enabled her to send troops and equipment to the frontiers with great speed. The troop train (below) was hauled by an engine of the Prussian–Hessian State Lines. Many old engines had been stored away for use in the war.

German troop train

The French troop train (right) was made up of covered wagons with open slatted sides. These were labeled *'Hommes quarante — chevaux huit.'* (That is, 40 men or 8 horses.) Guns and wagons were carried on the flat open cars.

French troop train

Heavy artillery guns (right) were sometimes mounted on railroad tracks which allowed them to be advanced or withdrawn at maximum speed. They were often camouflaged or hidden in woods or tunnels. They were one answer to air attack.

The first British armored train (below) was built in the London and North Western Railway workshops at Crewe. The engine, in the middle, was a sturdy Great Northern 0-6-2 tank. At each end were naval quick firing guns, with provision for machine guns and riflemen in between. These trains were intended for coast defense, but never went into action.

World War I

In World War I (1914–18) trains were used to bring troops and supplies to the front. The railroads inevitably became targets for attack: bridges were destroyed, tunnel roofs were brought down, and tracks were torn up.

When the Germans advanced into Russia they were faced with a break of gauge, so they laid a standard gauge third rail as they advanced.

On the Western Front heavy rail-mounted artillery was used by each side, for long range bombardments from behind the lines. This artillery included the famous "Big Bertha" guns.

Germany and Austria had all the materials they needed to maintain their railroads. France, on the other hand, had to call on Great Britain for supplies of coal since most of her coal mines were in enemy hands.

The British Government nationalized the railroads for the whole of the war. Public services were reduced and speeds were cut because more stops were introduced into the schedules. Maintenance was reduced by painting out the different colors and the polished brass and copper.

A special service of coal trains to supply the ships of the British Grand Fleet based off the north coast of

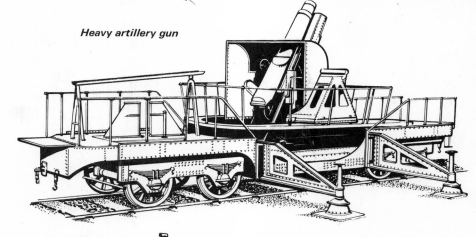

Heavy artillery gun

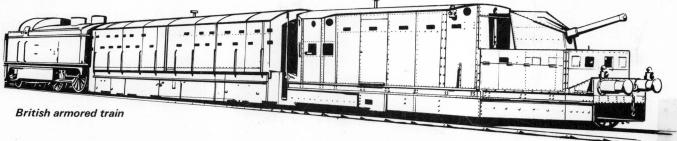

British armored train

As the war progressed, more and more British and American air raids from England were made against the railroads in German occupied France. Many sections of line were put out of action completely, often because of direct attacks to destroy the bridges. The supplies themselves were also often destroyed, such as the highly explosive cargo of ammunition trains and oil wagons (left).

Air attack in occupied France

The railroad bridge over the Thames River at Charing Cross (left) received a direct hit from a flying bomb. It had to be partly rebuilt because of damage to the main girders.
To combat interruptions to rail traffic, well equipped emergency repair squads were trained and held at various points. They could quickly clear away debris, relay track and restore signal and telephone communications.

Bomb damage on Charing Cross Bridge, London

Scotland was operated over the long and difficult single line of the Scottish Highland Railway.

Hospital trains and train ferries

Troop, armored, and hospital trains were made. The first hospital trains were converted from luggage vans. Later they were better equipped, with operating theaters for emergency cases.

Hospital trains, engines, and many wagons were sent to France. Train ferries were brought into service for this. The railroad cars had to be lifted aboard by cranes. At some ports special train ferry docks were built to overcome the change in tide level, so the train could be shunted straight on to the ship. Some years after the war the train ferries were used for regular passenger services.

World War II

In World War II (1939-45) railroads were used once again to move troops into strategic positions.

The British and Americans made a devastating air attack on the French railroads which were being used by the occupying German forces to bring up important supplies such as oil and ammunition. Bombing raids did tremendous damage both in England and Germany. Bridges, supply depots, marshaling yards and major junctions were all main targets. The damage affected both military and public services, which had to be cut back even further. After the war, it took many years to recover from all the damage and some of the services have never been restored.

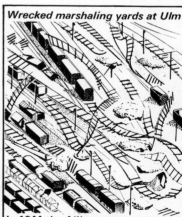

Wrecked marshaling yards at Ulm

In 1944 the Allies concentrated on destroying vital points on the enemy's railroads. The great marshaling yards at Ulm (above) were completely wrecked, so cutting off an important source of supplies to the German forces in France.

Railroads between the wars

Mail bag pick-up
The mail bag is hung from the post and is knocked off into a net by a passing mail train.

At the end of World War I in 1918 there was much damage that needed repairing on the railroads in many countries. This was an opportunity to develop and modernize the systems. Those countries that had a good supply of hydroelectric power, but no coal—such as Italy, Sweden and Switzerland—began electrification of the main lines.

Many routes were opened or improved with the building of new bridges and tunnels.

In 1931, the first unbroken transcontinental route across Africa from east to west, was completed.

New types of engine

Many new and powerful engines were designed to provide fast modern services. In Denmark the first diesel engines were developed in 1929 and in the 30's diesel railcars were providing regular services in the U.S. In 1932 a very powerful turbine locomotive came into use for hauling the heavy iron ore trains in Sweden. In Britain, new classes of steam engines were introduced, including the powerful 'Pacific' type of the 30's. In 1938 the engine *Mallard* reached 126 mph. This was the maximum speed ever reached by a steam locomotive.

In 1929, powerful 'Pacific' type engines were used on the New York, New Haven and Hartford Railroad which runs along the beautiful New England coast (right). In the 30's diesel services began in the United States.

'Pacific' engine,
New York, New Haven and Hartford Railroad

Canadian Pacific express

Frontier Mail train, India, Bombay, Baroda and Central India Railway

Cornish Riviera Express,
Great Western Railway

Flying Scotsman, London and North Eastern Railway

Rheingold Express

One of the most luxurious German passenger trains was the *Rheingold Express* (left). It was run by the *Mitropa Company* which was the German equivalent of the Wagon-Lits and Pullman services. This particular engine was a Bavarian 'Pacific'.

In 1933 the German State Railroad started a fast inter-city service with two-car diesel units. The first train was called the *Flying Hamburger*.

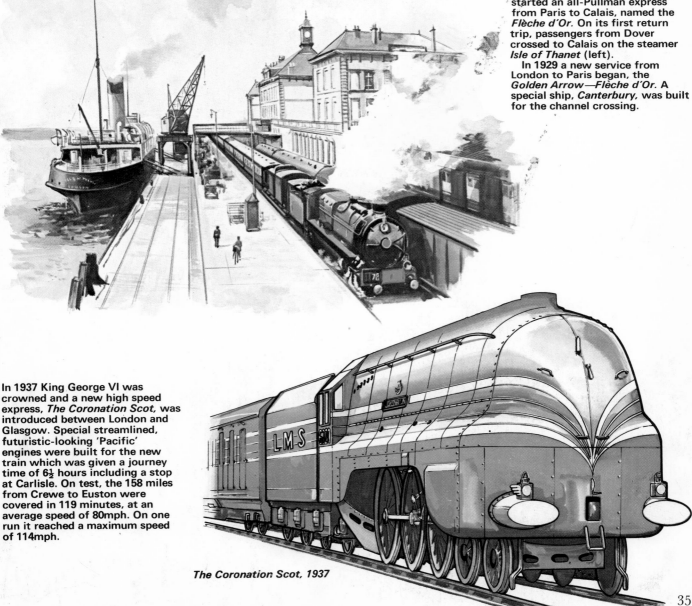

Flèche d'Or, 1926

In 1926 the Nord railroad of France started an all-Pullman express from Paris to Calais, named the *Flèche d'Or.* On its first return trip, passengers from Dover crossed to Calais on the steamer *Isle of Thanet* (left).

In 1929 a new service from London to Paris began, the *Golden Arrow—Flèche d'Or.* A special ship, *Canterbury*, was built for the channel crossing.

In 1937 King George VI was crowned and a new high speed express, *The Coronation Scot,* was introduced between London and Glasgow. Special streamlined, futuristic-looking 'Pacific' engines were built for the new train which was given a journey time of 6½ hours including a stop at Carlisle. On test, the 158 miles from Crewe to Euston were covered in 119 minutes, at an average speed of 80mph. On one run it reached a maximum speed of 114mph.

The Coronation Scot, 1937

Diesel and electric trains

The end of steam
Steam is now a thing of the past, although, as late as 1960, it was still possible to see a wood-burning steam engine and a diesel working side by side in Finland.

Diesel-electric engines are now common all over the world. They generate their own electricity and are not dependent on an external power supply.

Electricity offers three advantages. It affords rapid acceleration from rest, it gives full power at low speeds, and electrically powered engines do not need as much attention as steam engines. But an electric power unit is not self-contained, and if the power supply fails, everything comes to a halt. Electric engines are used for big and heavy trains, but lighter traffic is often worked by multiple units. These are made up of a number of cars each having one motor bogie, supplemented by ordinary coaches. Multiple units are useful for suburban or secondary services which run fairly slowly. But at high speed imperfectly synchronized motors along the train create a 'porpoising' effect, while a heavy motor bogie can make the lighter end of a coach 'wag its tail.' This is uncomfortable for the passengers.

Electrification in Europe
Electrification began with suburban services, but countries like Switzerland who had no coal, harnessed their waterfalls to generate electricity: others followed suit. Most European countries now have most of their lines electrified, France being one of the most advanced.

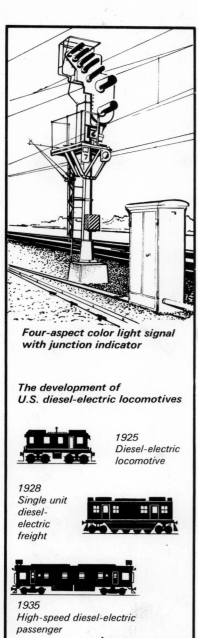

Four-aspect color light signal with junction indicator

The development of U.S. diesel-electric locomotives

1925 Diesel-electric locomotive

1928 Single unit diesel-electric freight

1935 High-speed diesel-electric passenger

1946 Diesel-electric narrow gauge

1955 6000hp rolling laboratory

1960 2500hp locomotive

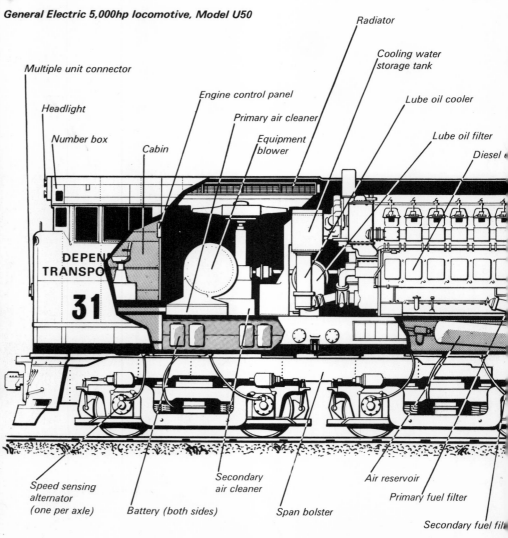

General Electric 5,000hp locomotive, Model U50

Multiple unit connector
Headlight
Number box
Cabin
Engine control panel
Primary air cleaner
Equipment blower
Radiator
Cooling water storage tank
Lube oil cooler
Lube oil filter
Diesel
Speed sensing alternator (one per axle)
Battery (both sides)
Secondary air cleaner
Span bolster
Air reservoir
Primary fuel filter
Secondary fuel fil

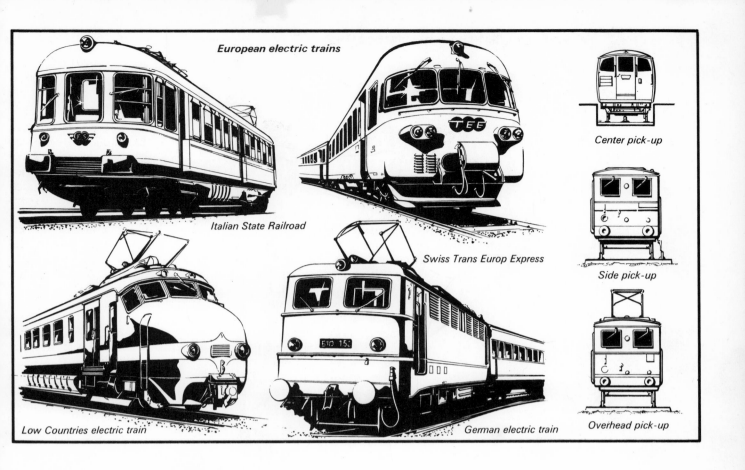

European electric trains

Italian State Railroad

Swiss Trans Europ Express

Low Countries electric train

German electric train

Center pick-up

Side pick-up

Overhead pick-up

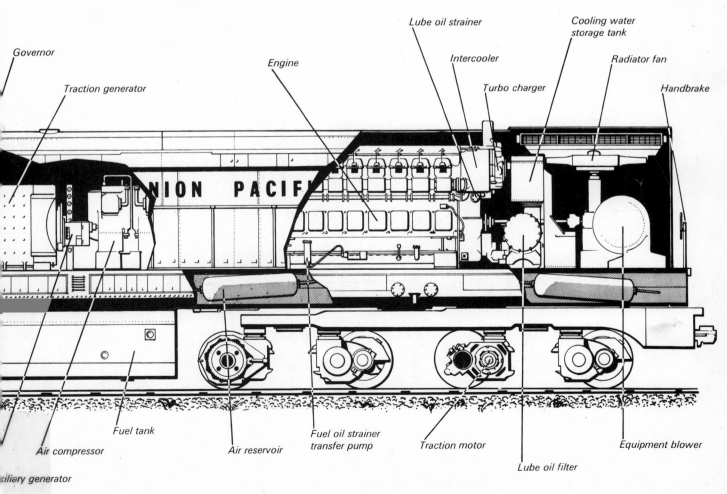

Governor

Traction generator

Engine

Lube oil strainer

Intercooler

Turbo charger

Cooling water storage tank

Radiator fan

Handbrake

Fuel tank

Air compressor

Auxiliary generator

Air reservoir

Fuel oil strainer transfer pump

Traction motor

Lube oil filter

Equipment blower

Modern trains since World War II

Moscow subway,
opened in 1938

By the beginning of this century many suburban railroads services were being replaced by electric streetcars and by buses. Passenger traffic declined as the number of private cars increased. Trucks were transporting freight that had previously gone by rail.

After World War II most countries closed those lines which did not pay. The first to go were the narrow gauge 'feeder lines.'

Railroad companies are now concentrating on providing efficient high speed services between important centers. In Europe, the Trans Europ Expresses (TEE) connect capitals and other important centers in every country. At Port Bau, on the frontier between France and Spain, the 4ft 8½in standard gauge meets the 5ft 6in Spanish gauge. All the wheels of *Le Catalan-Talgo* express from Barcelona to Geneva have to be changed.

Regular fast freight services are provided by liner trains. They transport raw materials and finished goods such as automobiles. Container trains carry giant packing cases which can be transferred intact on to trucks, which saves handling time.

France rebuilt her railroads after World War II and became the leader in modern reconstruction. A new *Mistral* express ran from Paris to Marseilles and the Riviera. On a special test one of the new engines reached a speed of 205mph—a world record. This train (right) is now included in the TEE network.

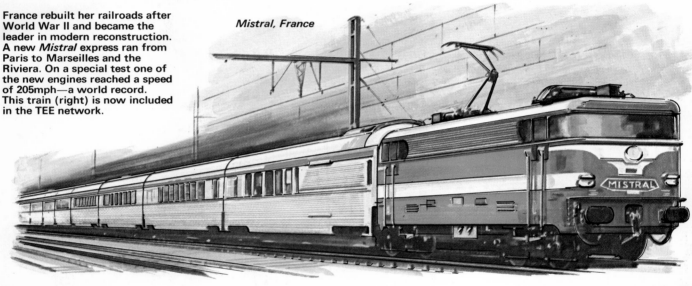

Mistral, France

One of Germany's efficient and comfortable trains is *The Rembrandt* (right) which runs from Amsterdam to Mannheim, where it divides. One portion goes on to Munich and the other to Zurich. The engine can develop 11,046hp. The train is superbly equipped. It is possible for passengers to telephone any part of the world from it.

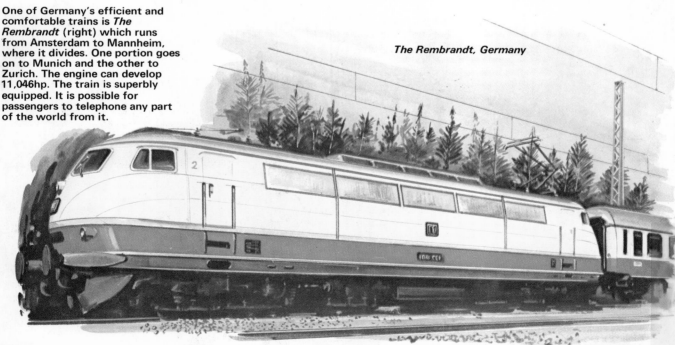

The Rembrandt, Germany

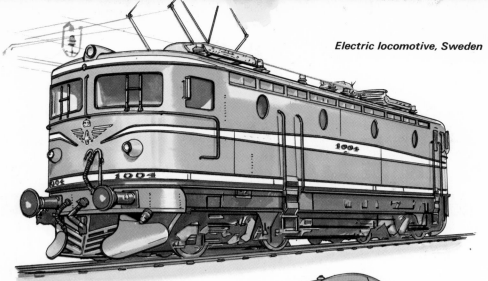

Electric locomotive, Sweden

In Sweden many of the lines are electrified. The engine (left) has high power but is light in weight. Swedish railroads connect with West Germany and Denmark by train ferries.

Diesel locomotive, Denmark

A modern diesel-electric engine (left) built in Sweden for the Danish State Railways.
There are many islands in Denmark. The larger ones are connected by train ferry services.

Mediolanum, Italy

Another high speed train of the TEE network is the Italian *Mediolanum* (left) which runs from Milan to Munich. The 357 miles take just over eight hours. This is a very good run because there is a fairly steep climb over the Brenner Pass between Italy and Austria.

Nielsen Cable Railway, Switzerland

Aerial cableway, France

The Neilsen Cable Railway (far left) in Switzerland climbs about 5,400ft. It is one of the steep, narrow gauge lines on which the cable cars are moved by one common cable between the rails.

Aerial cableways have also been built in mountainous regions to bridge chasms and scale vertical heights. A cable car in the Mont Blanc area (left) crosses a 4,430ft gap, suspended 1,000ft above the ground.

The fastest train in the World Japan

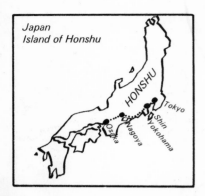

Map of Japan showing the route of the New Tokaido Line from Tokyo to Osaka and some of the twelve stops.

The super-express train (below) of the New Tokaido Line from Tokyo to Osaka, passes near Mount Fujiyama. Known as the *Hikari* expresses, these are the fastest trains in the world.

The New Tokaido line

Japan is a highly developed country with a large population. The existing 3ft 6in gauge rail system was not adequate so a new 4ft 8½in standard gauge line has been built from Tokyo to Osaka. It has been such a success since it was opened in 1964 that further extensions of the high speed standard gauge lines will be introduced in the future.

Japan's amazing Hikari

On the old line, trains averaged only 68mph with many stops. The new line has been built for directness and speed. It is elevated throughout and there are many bridges. So there are no crossings or steep gradients. Speeds of over 130mph are normal and speeds of 159mph are now being developed. This makes these the fastest trains in the world. There are 12 stops and the time for the whole 340-mile journey is 3 hours 10 minutes. This more than halves the best time on the old route, of 6 hours 30 minutes.

Automatic train control is used throughout, instead of conventional signaling. Electrical power is picked up from overhead wires.

Hikari, the fastest train in the world

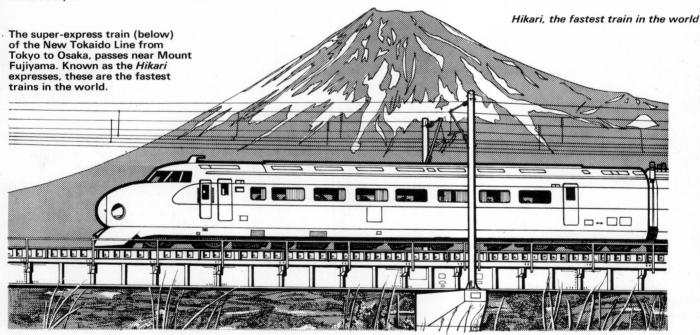

The driver (right) checks the control panel and instruments before starting. There are no signals on the route because there is completely automatic train control.

The interior of a third class coach (far right) on the *Kadoma Limited* express on the New Tokaido Line.

Engine control panel

Interior of a super-express train car

Australia's new transcontinental train

When a standard gauge working was recently made possible all across Australia a train of an entirely new concept was built for the new service. The *Indian Pacific* runs twice a week from the Indian Ocean shore at Perth to Sydney harbor on the Pacific, and it takes 65 hours for the 2,461 miles. Traveling easily and comfortably by train has become very popular in Australia and is also becoming more and more attractive to overseas visitors. It provides strong competition to the airlines.

The train is regarded as a traveling hotel and it comprises well equipped compartments complete with showers and toilets—equal to many found on board ship—and in the daytime the beds are transformed into comfortable armchairs. There is a very good observation lounge, a cocktail lounge, a music room, and a dining room where the five course meals, which are included in the fare, are served.

The route runs straight across the Great Nullabor Plain which is partly in Western and partly in South Australia. It includes the longest dead straight piece of track in the world, 328 miles long.

Map of Australia showing the route of the new transcontinental *Indian Pacific* express and the connections to Brisbane and Sydney.

Interior of lounge car

Cafeteria/club car

The interior of a first class lounge car (far left) on the *Indian Pacific* express, complete with piano and radiogram.

The interior of a cafeteria/club car (left) which is open to both first and second class passengers.

Indian Pacific Express

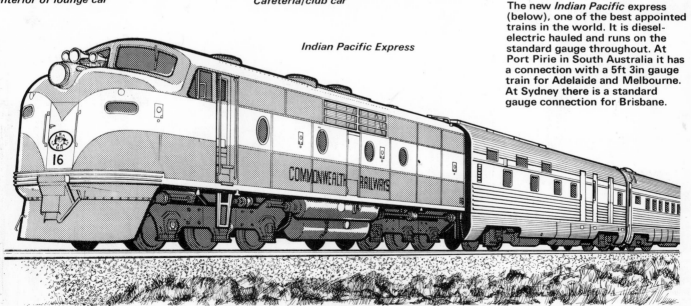

The new *Indian Pacific* express (below), one of the best appointed trains in the world. It is diesel-electric hauled and runs on the standard gauge throughout. At Port Pirie in South Australia it has a connection with a 5ft 3in gauge train for Adelaide and Melbourne. At Sydney there is a standard gauge connection for Brisbane.

Railroad curiosities past and future

Rigi mountain railroad

Most mountain railroads are too steep to work by normal adhesion —the wheels would not grip the rails. So a cable, or rack and pinion, is used to assist in haulage. On the Rigi mountain railroad (right) in Switzerland, a strong toothed rack is laid between the rails. An engaging cog or gear wheel, called a pinion, is fitted under the engine to help in pulling or braking.

This line is narrow gauge and very slow, but there are places where main lines are rack and pinion assisted, such as over the Andes mountains, between Argentina and Chile.

Ballybunion monorail

The Listowel and Ballybunion line in Ireland was called a monorail but it was really a trestled line. There was a carrying rail at the top and lower lines for steadying on each side. The trains (right) were in fact panniers. They did not last for long.

Barmen-Elberfeld electric monorail

An electric monorail (right) with the cars hung from an overhead rail was built from Barmen to Elberfeld in West Germany. It provided a local service throughout both World Wars.

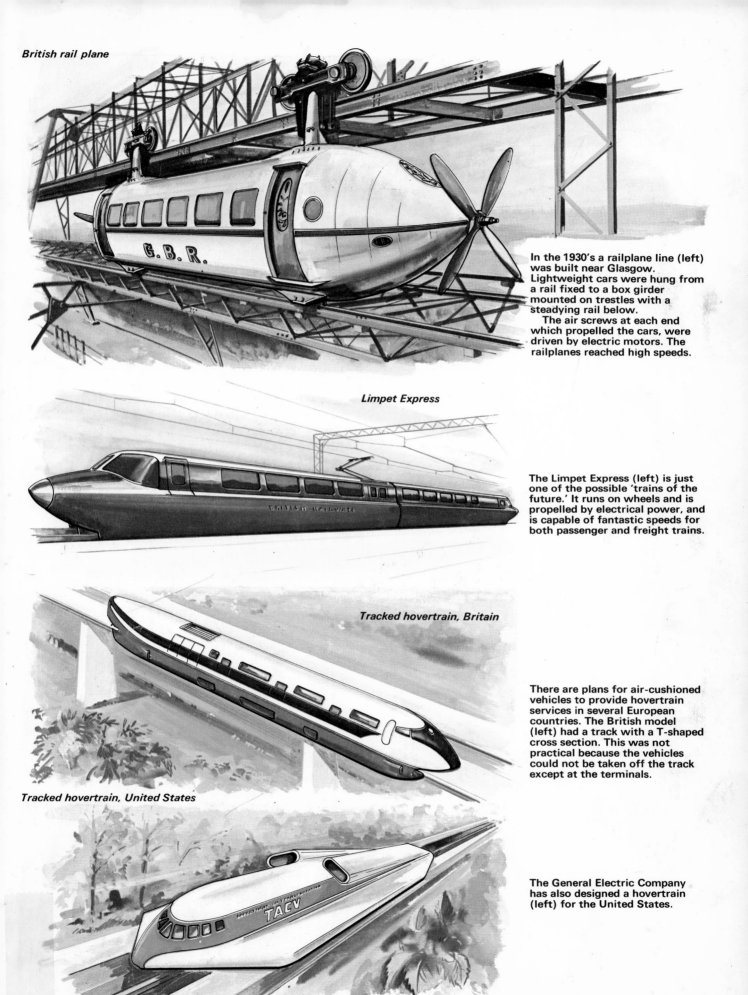

British rail plane

G.B.R.

In the 1930's a railplane line (left) was built near Glasgow. Lightweight cars were hung from a rail fixed to a box girder mounted on trestles with a steadying rail below.

The air screws at each end which propelled the cars, were driven by electric motors. The railplanes reached high speeds.

Limpet Express

The Limpet Express (left) is just one of the possible 'trains of the future.' It runs on wheels and is propelled by electrical power, and is capable of fantastic speeds for both passenger and freight trains.

Tracked hovertrain, Britain

There are plans for air-cushioned vehicles to provide hovertrain services in several European countries. The British model (left) had a track with a T-shaped cross section. This was not practical because the vehicles could not be taken off the track except at the terminals.

Tracked hovertrain, United States

TACV

The General Electric Company has also designed a hovertrain (left) for the United States.

Projects

Cable 'railways'

In mountainous countries the only suitable form of local 'railroad' is a cable car. Here a strong steel cable replaces the rails, and the car is suspended from it in such a manner that it can be hauled along. A single length of cable can sometimes run from one mountain top to another, or across a deep ravine. Usually, the cable car runs up the side of a mountain, with the cable suspended at intervals from steel towers.

Cable cars can ascend very steep gradients, which makes them quite different from railroads which have to run over more or less level ground. They travel only slowly, as this reduces the amount of power needed to winch the car up and down the cable.

This model will show how a cable car system works.

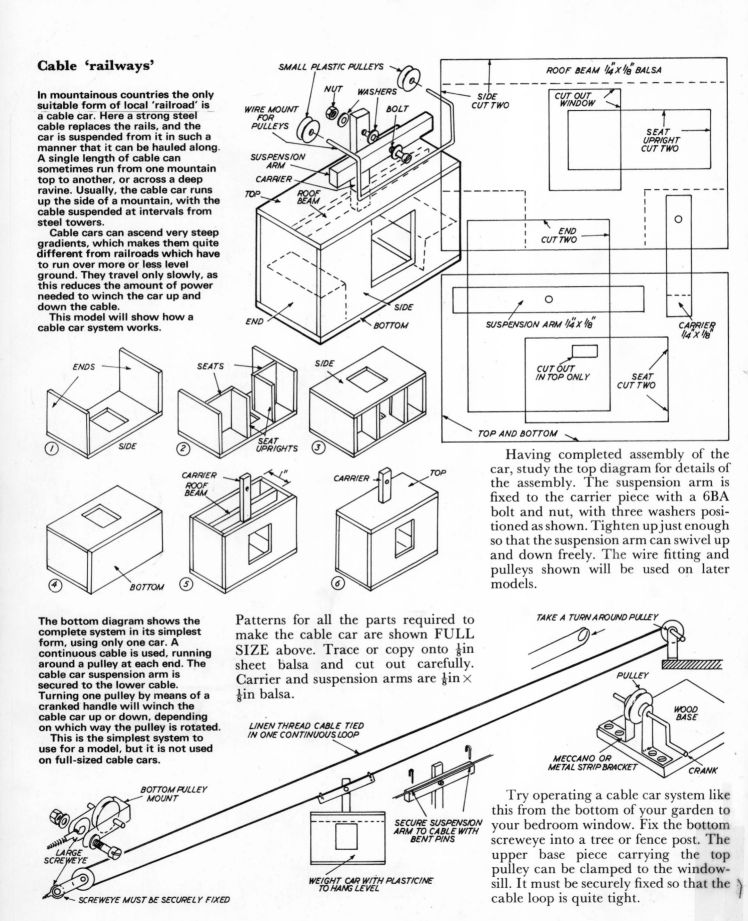

SMALL PLASTIC PULLEYS
NUT WASHERS
WIRE MOUNT FOR PULLEYS
BOLT
SUSPENSION ARM
CARRIER
TOP
ROOF BEAM
END
SIDE
BOTTOM

ROOF BEAM 1/4" X 1/8" BALSA
SIDE CUT TWO
CUT OUT WINDOW
SEAT UPRIGHT CUT TWO
END CUT TWO
SUSPENSION ARM 1/4" X 1/8"
CARRIER 1/4" X 1/8"
CUT OUT IN TOP ONLY
SEAT CUT TWO
TOP AND BOTTOM

① ENDS SIDE
② SEATS SEAT UPRIGHTS
③ SIDE
④ BOTTOM
⑤ CARRIER ROOF BEAM 1"
⑥ CARRIER TOP

Having completed assembly of the car, study the top diagram for details of the assembly. The suspension arm is fixed to the carrier piece with a 6BA bolt and nut, with three washers positioned as shown. Tighten up just enough so that the suspension arm can swivel up and down freely. The wire fitting and pulleys shown will be used on later models.

The bottom diagram shows the complete system in its simplest form, using only one car. A continuous cable is used, running around a pulley at each end. The cable car suspension arm is secured to the lower cable. Turning one pulley by means of a cranked handle will winch the cable car up or down, depending on which way the pulley is rotated.

This is the simplest system to use for a model, but it is not used on full-sized cable cars.

Patterns for all the parts required to make the cable car are shown FULL SIZE above. Trace or copy onto $\frac{1}{8}$in sheet balsa and cut out carefully. Carrier and suspension arms are $\frac{1}{8}$in × $\frac{1}{8}$in balsa.

LINEN THREAD CABLE TIED IN ONE CONTINUOUS LOOP

TAKE A TURN AROUND PULLEY
PULLEY
WOOD BASE
MECCANO OR METAL STRIP BRACKET
CRANK

BOTTOM PULLEY MOUNT
LARGE SCREWEYE
SCREWEYE MUST BE SECURELY FIXED

SECURE SUSPENSION ARM TO CABLE WITH BENT PINS
WEIGHT CAR WITH PLASTICINE TO HANG LEVEL

Try operating a cable car system like this from the bottom of your garden to your bedroom window. Fix the bottom screweye into a tree or fence post. The upper base piece carrying the top pulley can be clamped to the window-sill. It must be securely fixed so that the cable loop is quite tight.

This is a simplified model of the system normally used for cable cars. A separate cable is used for *suspension*, stretched between two secure anchoring points. The suspension arm of the car is fitted with pulleys which run on this cable. A second *traction* cable is then used for winching the car up and down the suspension cable.

SUSPENSION CABLE STRETCHED BETWEEN TWO SECURE ANCHOR POINTS

TRACTION CABLE

BEND UP WIRE COTTON BINDING

TRACTION CABLE

PULLEY
WINCH
HANDLE
METAL BRACKET

TAKE CABLE TWO OR THREE TIMES AROUND WINCH ROLLER

SUSPENSION ARM SECURED TO CABLE

CAR 2

RETURN PULLEYS

CAR 1

WINCH

CAR 2

SUSPENSION CABLES

CAR 1

TRACTION CABLE

RETURN PULLEYS

Study pictures of full-sized cable cars and try to work out what sort of cable system they are using. For a start, count how many cables there are for each car. Then try to work out what happens to the cables at each end.

Fix two large screweyes to act as anchor points for the suspension cable and screw them home as tight as you can. Then tie the suspension cable tightly between them. Use thin fishing line, or the thin wire used for controlling model aircraft for this cable.

Bend the arm to take the suspension arm pulleys from fairly stout wire (e.g. 16 gauge galvanized iron wire). Bind it in place to the suspension arm, slip on the pulleys and turn the ends of the wire up to keep the pulleys in place.

You need a winch and pulley at each end this time, mounted in a metal bracket as shown with the pulley above the winch. A cotton spool makes a good winch, or you can use a short piece of dowel.

The *traction cable* connecting them can be of thread. Note that it is in two parts, running from the winch to the suspension arm of the car—but each length must be as long as the full length of the suspension cable.

The second system is more interesting because as one car is winched in one direction the other is moved in the opposite direction. On an inclined cable run, the weight of the car going down will help pull the other car upward. The system only uses one continuous cable—all right for a model, but not safe enough for a full-sized cable car.

The third system uses exactly the same cable layout for winching, but both cars are now supported on their own separate suspension cables, which is much safer. Another advantage of separate suspension cables is that the fixings for the pulleys carrying the traction cable are under far less strain.

A rack railroad

A rack-and-pinion railroad can climb very steep slopes without any danger of slipping back. The wheels still run on rails, but merely 'freewheel.' The drive is taken to a gear wheel under the center of the car, which engages with a rack—which is really like a lot of gear teeth laid out in a straight line. The drive gear wheel or *pinion* rotates very slowly and literally climbs up the *rack*, tooth by tooth. To descend, the pinion is rotated the other way, to climb down the rack.

MARK ENDS   SAW SLITS   CARVE GEAR TEETH

ABOUT 1/4"

CUT OFF END OF CANDLE AND PIERCE HOLE IN CENTRE

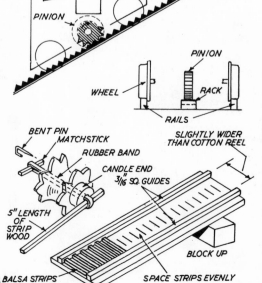

RACK

PINION

WHEEL   PINION   RACK

RAILS

BENT PIN
MATCHSTICK
RUBBER BAND

SLIGHTLY WIDER THAN COTTON REEL

CANDLE END
3/16" SQ. GUIDES

5" LENGTH OF STRIP WOOD

BLOCK UP

3/16" SQ. BALSA STRIPS   SPACE STRIPS EVENLY

The very simple climbing model shown demonstrates the non-slip properties of a rack-and-pinion drive. Find a large cotton spool, mark out each end with a number of equally spaced 'arms' and saw a slit down each arm. Then cut away into a V shape with a sharp knife until you have given the cotton spool 'gear teeth' ends. Try to get the shape of each 'tooth' as near the same as possible.

Make the rack from balsa wood, with guide rails and 'teeth' consisting of pieces of 3/16in square balsa glued at equal spacings between the guide rails.

Wind up the cotton reel 'gear' by rotating the wood arm in a counter-clockwise direction. Place at the bottom of the rack and watch it climb up, step by step, as the teeth engage the rack pieces one by one.

Planning a railroad schedule

To start with we will plan the schedule around just three trains—an Express, a Local (stopping) train and a Freight train.

Suppose we start the day at 06.00, with a local or stopping train leaving Maintown. Plot this out on the schedule, i.e.

Local depart *Maintown* from
platform 1 . . . .06.00
depart *Boston* 06.15
depart *Springfield* .06.30
depart *Greenfield* . .06.45
arrive *Southtown* on
platform 2 . . . .07.00

We also want a regular express service between *Maintown* and *Southtown*, running non-stop. The first express of the day is to leave *Maintown* at 07.00, arriving at *Southtown* at 07.30. Plot this on the schedule.

Start with the express, working it backwards and forwards between *Maintown* and *Southtown*. For example, having arrived at *Southtown* at 07.30, it can leave again at 08.00, arriving back at *Maintown* at 08.30. Allocate a suitable platform for it to arrive at. Now carry on planning the express runs through the day, as this is the most important passenger service. The local and freight trains can be worked in around the express schedule.

We have the local left at *Southtown*, having arrived at platform 2 at 07.00. There is another service from *Maintown* to *Southtown* following (the express), so delay departure of the local on its return trip until 07.45.

The local is now traveling back, but it is being followed by the express at 08.00, which is going to catch up with it. To clear the line the local can stop at platform 2 at *Greenfield* until 08.15.

However, the local will now arrive at *Boston* a little before 08.45 and the express is leaving *Maintown* again on the down trip at 09.00. Once again the local can be directed to platform 2 at *Boston* and held there until the express has passed through in the opposite direction. The local can then leave *Boston* at 09.15 and proceed to *Maintown*.

Carry on right through the day's plan in the same way.

We also need to work in some freight trains. These have to be slotted in between the passenger services.

This is a plan of an imaginary railroad system. It is designed for a single line working on the main line, since this provides more of a challenge when planning a schedule. Draw it out much larger on a sheet of paper. Trains can be represented by strips of balsa wood, laid in place over the plan and moved along the lines, at the times decided by your schedule.

For working the model—and planning the schedule—you need to adopt a "scale" for time. A time 'scale.' A good scale to use is one minute equals one hour. You then need a watch or clock with a second hand, so that you can read seconds as minutes.

With this time scale, 6 minutes would represent six hours, or 06.00. So 6 minutes 15 seconds would be 06.15 . . . 6 minutes 30 seconds would be 06.30, and so on. In this way you can cover a complete 24 hour day in 24 minutes actual working time.

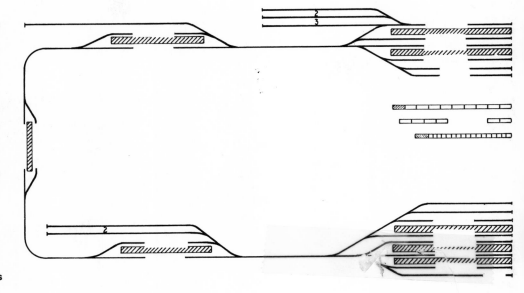

TIME					
06.00					
06.15					
06.30					
06.45					
07.00					
07.15					
07.30					
07.45					
08.00					
08.30					
08.45					
09.00					
09.15					
09.30					
09.45					
10.00					
10.15					
10.30					
10.45					
11.00					
11.15					
11.30					
11.45					
12.00					
12.15					
12.30					
12.45					
13.00					

Remember that when you end the day's schedules, both the express and local must end up back where they started from at the beginning of the day—otherwise you will be short of a train or trains to start the next day's schedule!

The working schedule plots out how a complete rail system is run, in both directions, with all types of trains. From this we can extract a timetable, which shows the passenger services in both directions. *Maintown* to *Southtown* is the 'down' run; and *Southtown* to *Maintown* the 'up' run. Separate timetables must be worked out for each.

Index

Numbers in italics refer to illustrations